vegetarian comfort food

vegetarian comfort food

meals like mom makes, without the meat

Jennifer Warren

whitecap

Vancouver/Toronto

Visit the Whitecap Books website at www.whitecap.ca

Edited by Alison Maclean
Copy edited by Elizabeth McLean
Proofread by Lesley Cameron
Cover and interior design by Maxine Lea
Illustrations by Joanna Mitchell
Author photo by Kate Fellerath

Printed and bound in Canada

National Library of Canada Cataloguing in Publication Data

Warren, Jennifer, 1976–
     Vegetarian comfort food

        Includes index.
        ISBN 1-55285-216-X

        1. Vegetarian cookery. I.Title.
TX837.W373 2001   641.5'636   C2001-910977-6

The publisher acknowledges the support of the Canada Council and the
Cultural Services Branch of the Government of British Columbia in making
this publication possible. We acknowledge the financial support of the
Government of Canada through the Book Publishing Industry Development
Program for our publishing activities.

dedication

To my mother and my father

contents

acknowledgments

This cookbook is my first, and as such it was a labor of love—for me as well as those close to me. This is why I am grateful to the following people:

Suzanne Brandreth, friend and agent, who had absolute faith in me and this book right from the start. Without her, this book would never have been cooked up, at least not in its present form. Which brings me to . . .

Robert McCullough, Alison Maclean, and Maxine Lea at Whitecap Books, who shared my vision for a fun, fabulous, useful book full of delicious vegetarian recipes.

My testers, tasters, and friends: Sarah Bonato, Rod Cartagena, Bob Dick, Tara Nelson, and Andrew, Donna, Joel, and Marcie Weitzman.

Eva Blank, math whiz, who helped me figure out the volume of a cylinder (you need to know these things when making up a cheesecake recipe).

Lesley Warren, Debbi Warren, Jennifer Bauer, Kate Fellerath, and Jeff Einboden for their pats on the back.

My extremely supportive boss, Greg Ioannou of Colborne Communications.

Ken and Catherine Cole, proprietors of The Great Vine Whole Foods in Huntsville, Ontario, for giving me the greatest job going through high school and university, and changing my life in the process.

My mom and dad, for raising me right—with no measuring cups anywhere to be seen, and food, pots, and pans everywhere.

Ilana Weitzman, for her unflagging love and help with the washing-up.

introduction

When I became vegetarian at seventeen, I still lived under my parents' roof. And deep down, I still expected to eat their cooking. This, in a nutshell, is why this book was written.

Both my mom and dad are fabulous cooks, as anyone who visits their Muskoka, Ontario, restaurant knows. But their repertoire—full of shepherd's pies and stews, rich gravies, and mixed grills—contained few meatless dishes, leaving me with no choice but to tackle the kitchen myself.

What to eat? What to cook? Stymied, I started buying up the best-looking vegetarian cookbooks I could find. My mom looked over my shoulder in growing concern as I leafed through page after page of intricate, difficult-to-prepare, and ultimately bland and unsatisfying food. Her brow furrowed. Where were the good, hearty, savory dishes she had fed me as a kid? And more importantly, where were the trifles, cakes, and rice pudding? How would her daughter maintain her rosy cheeks without custard?

I was faithful to these cookbooks for the first little while—I didn't have much choice. I suffered through soymilk taste-tests, shopping trips for various unrefined grains, and repetitive bean-soaking. Scoops of falafel mix whirled above my head in nightmares, crowned by gloppy squirts of tahini. Meanwhile, my parents puzzled. Would I bend over tasteless stir-fries for the rest of my life, adding more five-spice powder and garlic and doubling the recipe's soy sauce quotient in desperation? After my first year of vegetarianism, my parents shook their heads in bewilderment. Their daughter was eating hippie food.

I never doubted my decision to become vegetarian. But I certainly didn't have much fun in that first year.

My mom and dad took over when I turned yellowish and grim-looking. Familiar smells began to waft from the kitchens of our house and our restaurant. My parents somehow managed to recreate a few of my favorite dishes, and this inspired me to start creating my own. After seven years of this, I've written this book.

What is "comfort cooking"? When we think of comfort food, we probably think of casseroles, mashed potatoes—foods that are made at home with family, rather than chosen off the menu at a posh, stiff restaurant.

You may have noticed, however, that this is not a casserole cookbook. This is because *my* idea of comfort cooking is, quite simply, whatever foods make me happy—when preparing them, when serving them to others, and when eating them. We don't always seek comfort in the same thing. Some nights we'll crave a good pasta, while others we'll want something completely different. This is why you'll find a variety of recipes in this book.

Comfort cooking also means food that makes us happy without fussy presentation. I'm not a flashy person and I'm not a showy cook. I look upon intricate little towers of food, garnished with some sort of leaf, with distrust. I'm more concerned with the way something tastes than with whether the asparagus spears are arranged into a perfect sunburst formation. As such, I don't give a lot of instruction about garnishes or arrangement, unless I've thought of something fairly low-fuss and quick. And from what I've heard first-hand from my brother—who is a chef with his own catering business—when those gourmets come home from a long day of color-coding ingredients and making delightful little fans out of things, all they want to do is sit down with a big bowl of macaroni and cheese, because that's what makes them feel at home.

To me, another important feature of comfort cooking is that it pays homage to the classics. This applies both to the finished dish and the techniques employed in its preparation. In order to cook really well, you need to learn some fundamental things: why a roux is used for sauces, how to melt chocolate properly, and how to make a custard, to name a few. Once I had these abilities, I could go on to make things that had only been within the grasp of my mom or dad: white sauce, chocolate cakes, and sherry trifle, for instance.

This book is also the product of my obsession with foods that went "out" before my time, or foods that were going out as I came in. When I cook for others, my food is often met with a delighted, "No one makes that anymore!" And it's true. I think that this is also an attribute of comfort food—it reminds the people enjoying it of another time, perhaps of their own childhood.

It's probably an odd combination—recipes that are retro *and* vegetarian—but it works for me, and it seems to delight those around me. Much of my inspiration as a cook comes from my collection of vintage cookbooks from the '50s and '60s, with their fabulous technicolor photos and ethos of wonderfully satisfying, and somewhat whimsical, family food. Potato salad, glazed carrots, apple crumble—it's all in here, and it's delicious.

Instead of hunting out that quarter teaspoon of impossible-to-locate spice, I strive to cook with good, easy-to-find ingredients with a minimum of fuss and bother. Accordingly, most of the ingredients in this book are common and simple to locate.

However, some recipes do call for a certain magic vegetarian ingredient. In these cases, I've included a description of the ingredient—as well as likely places to find it—in the Glossary of Ingredients and Cooking Terms at the end of the book. I can guarantee you won't have to go farther than your bulk or health food store to find it.

Most of the recipes in this book will feed four to six hungry people—really. With vegetarian food, much of the work is usually in the chopping and preparing of ingredients. Or, as my mom has often said: once you get the kitchen in a right mess, you might as well save yourself having to do it all again tomorrow.

So, even if you're cooking for one or two, the leftovers can make a convenient and quick meal. Should you have a large family, a desire for a fully stocked freezer, or a serious dinner party on your hands, the recipes can be very easily doubled, tripled, and so on. If you happen to hate leftovers, you will find that these recipes, for the most part, can be halved easily.

The dishes in this book are generally very easy to prepare. The more complicated dishes, such as Cabbage Rolls or Mini Breakfast Quiches, are simply a few more steps rather than a lot more difficult. My brother and dad may be trained professionals, but I am not. I have little patience for failure-prone foods. That said, a few things require a bit more dexterity and cunning. For example, don't serve the Cherries Jubilee on a night when you do not feel capable of safely setting something on fire.

I hope that the recipes in this book give you faith in how satisfying and delicious vegetarian food can be. I hope you read the book for fun, the way I do with my favorite cookbooks, and riff off my ideas, coining your own masterpieces. I also hope that, through your creative cooking, you inspire other people to become vegetarian.

The recipes in this book will help you become a hale and hearty vegetarian. But they are also deeply enjoyable and soul-satisfying. And isn't that what comfort cooking should be all about?

basics

Basics

The more you cook, the more you learn. I think that previous generations cooked a lot more than ours does and, as a result, a lot of us grew up without knowing about basic cookery techniques and proper ingredients. In the recipes, I try to explain myself as clearly as possible so that you aren't left scratching your head. However, some things just didn't fit into the recipes—and that's why they're here.

On Reading Recipes

When you're about to use a recipe, take the time to read through the whole thing, from introduction to ingredients to method to yield, **before you start doing anything**. This will give you a holistic picture of the recipe so that you can get all of your ingredients, bowls, and cooking tools together before you start. It will also give you an idea of how many "breaks" you have in between steps, and how long those breaks are. It's terrible to let the garlic burn as you furiously look for the can opener for the tomatoes.

A Chopping Primer

When you're cooking vegetarian, cutting up your vegetables into various little bits is usually the most time-consuming thing you have to do. But how little should the bits be? Here are some general rules.

Chop: Cut into pieces about $^1/_2$ inch (1 cm) wide.

Coarsely Chop: Cut into larger, more irregular pieces. Usually, you coarsely chop things only when they're going to be puréed.

Finely Chop: Cut into pieces about $^1/_4$ inch (.5 cm) wide.

Dice: Cut vegetables into cubes about $^1/_3$–$^1/_2$ inch (.8–1 cm) square.

Julienne: Cut into pieces just slightly thicker than wooden matches.

Mince: Cut as small as you can, so that actual pieces of the food are hardly perceptible. A mince is much finer than a fine chop.

Shred: Use your knife to very finely slice something with a lot of layers—like cabbage for coleslaw.

Slice: Cut vertically from top to bottom, as you would bread.

Diagonal Slice: This is usually for long, round things like carrots. Slice on an angle, so that your slices are longer and larger, but not thicker.

Generally, it's a good idea to chop your ingredients before you start cooking. There are exceptions to this rule, however. If you have to simmer something for 15 minutes before adding the next ingredient, use that time to chop that next ingredient. And never chop pears, apples, or avocados until right before cooking, blending, or serving—they discolor quickly.

The Stuff You Should Buy

What makes a good vegetarian cook? Perseverance, creativity . . . and a really good food processor. I should say that, as far as relying on kitchen gadgets goes, I'm somewhere in the middle of the road. I love my lemon reamer and would never give it up, but I draw the line at garlic-peeling mats and "Rotatoes." Here are the pieces of kit that I use all the time, as well as those that I find extremely useful on a less frequent basis.

Knives

Vegetarian cooks spend a lot of time chopping, slicing, and dicing. Invest in a few good knives to make your job easier. The essentials are a large chef's knife, a long serrated knife, and a small paring knife. These can be "self-sharpening" knives that come in their own sharpening holder—but if they're not, buy a knife sharpener as well.

Pots and Pans

You should have a small saucepan for melting butter, a medium saucepan for boiling vegetables and simmering sauces, and a large saucepan for making soup and cooking pasta. These should all have lids.

You should have a large and a small skillet that are each at least 2 inches (5 cm) deep. I use skillets with a non-stick coating, because I find that these make flipping and removing foods much easier, and I also use less butter and oil. If you love cast iron or another such sticky type, increase the butter and oil in the recipes.

You should have a deep wok or a pan that is shaped like a wok—this is great for stir-fries and sauces. Mine is a wok-like pan with a non-stick coating, which I find makes my stir-fries less oily.

Things That Go in the Oven

Many department stores have boxed sets that include the basic things you need for baking: two round cake pans (for layer cakes), a muffin pan, a loaf pan, and one or two cookie sheets.

A good pie plate is not much money—a heavy glass one is about $10—so please buy one and don't rely on those terrible, flimsy, disposable aluminum things you buy in the grocery store. They don't cook as evenly and they make your great creation look cheap.

As well, keep an eye out at garage sales and thrift stores for good casserole and baking dishes—or if you're more uppity, check out department store sales. Pyrex and other heavy glass dishes, square or rectangular, are excellent buys because you can make many different things in them, from cakes to casseroles.

Stirring and Flipping

You need the right weapons to mix, sauté, beat, blend, and fry. Wooden or melamine spoons with long handles are a must for soups and sauces, but stick to melamine for baking—melamine doesn't pick up flavors like wood does.

Spatulas of different types are very useful for flipping pancakes and serving cakes and squares—just make sure you buy durable plastic or melamine rather than metal if you have non-stick pans. Also, invest in one or two rubber scrapers to get every last bit of cake batter or whipped cream out of your bowl (if your child, pet, or roommate doesn't beat you to it).

A whisk is a good investment for beating eggs as well as making cream sauces smooth.

Cutting Boards

Whether you use wood or plastic is up to you, but I recommend you have at least two cutting boards. Knight one as "the onion and garlic board," on which you can chop other savory ingredients as well. Don't ever use the other cutting board for onions or garlic—this way, you'll have one board that can always be used for chopping fruit or chocolate without having garlicky, bizarre-tasting pies or cakes.

Mixing Bowls

Buy a few of varying sizes—this will make your job much easier when cooking, allowing you to mix on without worrying about washing up. Try to buy good-quality stainless steel or heavy heatproof glass. Plastic can pick up food odors and it can warp when exposed to heat, so it's best to avoid it.

Whizzers

I love my blender and food processor. Though I'm not one of those savvy cooks who makes pastry in my machine as yet, I do use these wondrous appliances for blending soups, puréeing vegetables, and making salad dressings. You don't really need both of these appliances, but if you're choosing one I would tell you to go with the food processor. A blender works well for liquid-based things, so it's fine for soups and sauces. It's also less expensive. A food processor is more versatile, as it works better with non-liquidy things such as pestos and thick dips, and it grinds oats and nuts wonderfully, as well as doing most of the things that a blender does.

If you're interested in whipping up cream and meringues, as I am, an electric mixer is another good investment. It's also excellent for creaming together butter, sugar, and eggs for cookies and squares.

Strainers

The essentials are a large colander for draining pasta and cooked vegetables, and a fine-mesh sieve for sifting flour and cocoa.

Other Helpers

Various and sundry tools, bits, and pieces:

- measuring cups and spoons
- can opener
- lemon reamer
- cheese slicer
- garlic press
- pizza-cutting wheel
- grater
- corkscrew
- vegetable peeler
- tongs
- potato masher
- ladle
- pastry brush
- salad spinner
- pastry blender
- pie server

Ingredients, or What Comes Out Is What Goes In

When I was broke and in university, I scrimped a lot on ingredients for cooking—buying the cheapest canned tomatoes and using terrible homemade wine for tomato sauce—you get the picture. I could try to milk the pathos of this scenario for all it's worth, but instead I'll be honest and tell you that I could have afforded to buy those better ingredients, and my cooking would have been that much better as a result. It was just that my liquor budget was a bit more hefty during that period . . . Back to the point: when you're cooking vegetarian, you don't have to spend money on steaks or fresh seafood. So spend the money on really good basic ingredients, such as:

Extra Virgin Olive Oil

Whenever I say "olive oil" in this book (and I say it very often), I mean "extra virgin olive oil." Why use extra virgin? Because it's so much better. Olive oil can only be called "extra virgin" when it has met requirements set by the International Olive Oil Council (IOOC) concerning the extraction process, taste, aroma, and acidity.

Tomatoes

Don't buy the 89-cent can of tomatoes. Please. In this cookbook, a lot of canned tomatoes are used, and when you spend the extra 20–40 cents on a better quality can of Italian tomatoes, the recipes will taste better. Similarly, don't buy the cheapest fresh tomatoes, either. Especially in the fall and winter months, tomatoes can taste like spongy shadows of their proper selves. Take advantage of the harvest of lovely, fresh, flavorful tomatoes in the summertime, and buy tomatoes on the vine in the winter.

Herbs and Spices

It's a very good idea to have a well-stocked spice cupboard when you're cooking vegetarian—you never know when a pinch of nutmeg, paprika, or oregano will mean the difference between bland and delicious. When buying spices or herbs, freshness is key. Either buy at a busy bulk or gourmet food store, so that you know the merchandise is moving, or buy in the smallest possible container.

Stocks

Vegetable stock adds flavor to recipes, and for this reason I usually recommend adding vegetable stock instead of water to savory recipes. Of course, the very nicest stock to use is one you make yourself—I would recommend this especially for soups that you're planning to serve at a special dinner. There's a stock recipe at the end of this chapter.

But if it's 6:30 p.m., you've just come home from work, and you need to make dinner, it certainly makes sense to have some good instant stock lying around. When it comes to vegetarian stock powders and concentrates, read the labels. Even if you're buying your vegetable stock from a bulk bin, the staff should be able to find the ingredient list for you. What to look for?

- Your first ingredients should be vegetables, not oil.

- Sometimes, "vegetable stock" doesn't mean "vegetarian stock." Look for chicken and beef fat.

- Conversely, sometimes "chicken stock" doesn't have any actual chicken or chicken fat in it. Look at the ingredients as well as the name of the product. Usually these stock powders or concentrates will be called "imitation chicken stock" or "vegetarian chicken stock." Even though I generally use vegetable stock proper, I like to have some imitation chicken stock on hand because it really does lend a wonderfully homey taste to some sauces and dishes. For example, I prefer it to vegetable stock when making my Golden Mushroom Gravy (see page 82).

- Make sure that MSG isn't one of the first ingredients. Whether you choose one with MSG at all is up to you, but if you do, try to choose one that lists it as one of the last ingredients. For more information on MSG, look in the Glossary of Ingredients & Cooking Terms, at the back of the book.

On Fresh Breath

I use a lot of onions and garlic in this book. Fortunately, this is not such a problem as it would have been 10 or 20 years ago, when eating these flavor-giving plants was considered antisocial.

I don't really see why people should be nervous about onions and garlic. Why? First, I have cooked the recipes in this book many times for a lot of different people, and not once has anyone commented on the overriding flavor of these foods. (And I have some brutally honest people in my life.)

Second, I find that onions and garlic only have bad-breath-making powers when they're used raw. For that reason, I may use four cloves of garlic in a casserole that bakes for 30 minutes, but I only use one clove for a pesto that is uncooked. The same goes for onions. If you are hedging your bets on kissing someone after dinner, then cut down on the raw garlic or onions—but they shouldn't pose a problem when cooked.

Third, onions and garlic are good for you. Onions are very high in potassium and they're a good source of vitamin B$_6$. Garlic has been known throughout history for its medicinal purposes, and is believed by many to have antibiotic, immune-system-building properties. I use garlic in cooking all the time, and I get a cold only about every two years. Personally, I think there's a link there.

Substitutions—Notes for Vegans

Many of the recipes in this book use butter, milk, or eggs. In which recipes can you make vegan substitutions? Here are some guidelines:

Eggs

I have found eggs a real challenge to substitute successfully. However, there are now some quite good "egg replacers" on the market, including a particularly effective one that is a powder consisting of binders and leaveners—the two things that eggs do in baking. Do try them, and experiment.

Milk

In the last two years, the soymilks available on the market have risen dramatically in quality. I remember that when I became vegan, they were a light gray color with a distinctive beany taste, and they weren't available anywhere but the health food store. Now, soymilks are widely available at almost every grocery store and many of them are deliciously creamy, meaning that they can realistically be substituted for milk in all kinds of situations. (It is now also legal to fortify soymilks with calcium and nutrients, which is extremely important if you're trying to maintain a healthy dairy-free diet.) My advice would be to start with your favorite soymilk and experiment freely with it, or use rice or almond milk instead if you prefer these. These will probably be successful in most of the recipes in this book.

Butter

If you're making the switch from butter to margarine, here are a few notes on choosing a good one. First, try to find one that has as few chemicals in it as possible. I used to get one at the health food store that had no preservatives or color and was made with canola oil only, and it was very good. Also, just because it's margarine doesn't mean it's dairy-free. Many margarines have dairy ingredients in them, so read the label carefully to find one that's vegan if you're trying to skip dairy.

Once you've found a margarine that you like, go ahead and use it instead of butter for baking, greasing pans, etc. I would avoid using it for things like Asparagus in Lemon-Garlic Butter (p. 128) because you can't sub margarine for butter in a butter-based sauce. Also, I would recommend using olive oil rather than margarine when sautéing anything whatsoever—you're using butter in these cases for the flavor as well as the fat, and a good olive oil would be a lot tastier than margarine for this purpose.

Some Notes on Principles— For Vegans and the Rest of Us

Whether you're vegan or vegetarian, it's important to be informed about animal products and make your own decisions about what you are and aren't comfortable eating. When I became vegan, I did so because of factory farming—the practice of keeping animals such as cows and chickens in bunker-like living arrangements—which I see as extremely cruel and intolerable.

I was also very concerned about the quality of feed for the animals, as well as the use of antibiotics and medication.

Both of these concerns still exist for me, and as a vegetarian who has "lapsed" back into eating dairy and eggs, I try my best to purchase certified organic products, in which the feed is strictly regulated, or those produced on free-range farms where animals are not kept in horrendous tiny cages and stalls.

However, buying organic and free-range milk and eggs comes at a higher price, and you may not want to, or be able to, prioritize this extra expense. Read up on the subjects that interest or concern you and decide for yourself. Here are some resources that I recommend:

- *Diet for a Small Planet* by Frances M. Lappe
- *Diet for a New America* and *May All Be Fed: Diet for a New World* by John Robbins
- *Beyond Beef: The Rise and Fall of the Cattle Culture* by Jeremy Rifkin
- www.vegweb.com
- www.veg.org
- www.ivu.org
- www.vegansociety.com

In the past few years, information about veganism—including great recipes—has increased greatly. Do visit some of the websites I've listed above and take a look at their vegan recipes. You will find some excellent ones.

Vegetable Stock

A homemade vegetable stock makes a tremendous difference in cooking, if you have the time and inclination to make it. A real gourmet friend of mine makes large amounts of stock and then pours it into ice cube trays to freeze. After it's frozen, he dumps the cubes into resealable bags so that he can defrost only as much stock as he needs.

Makes about 10 cups (2.5 L)

12 cups	water	3 L
Essential Vegetables:		
3	large onions, coarsely chopped	3
6	cloves garlic, coarsely chopped	6
3	stalks celery, coarsely chopped	3
2	large carrots, coarsely chopped	2
1	potato, peeled and coarsely chopped, or 1 cup (250 mL) clean potato peelings	1
Optional Vegetables (must choose at least 2):		
2 cups	mushrooms, chopped	500 mL
2	leeks, greens removed and whites chopped	2
1 cup	green cabbage, coarsely chopped	250 mL
1 cup	rutabaga, coarsely chopped	250 mL
1 1/2 tsp.	salt	7.5 mL
6–8	black peppercorns	6–8
1	bay leaf	1
1 tsp.	thyme	5 mL

In a large saucepan, simmer onions and garlic with 1/2 tsp. (2.5 mL) salt and 1 cup (250 mL) of the water for 8–10 minutes, or until softened. Add the rest of the essential vegetables, as well as at least two of the optional vegetables. Add the rest of the water and salt, with the peppercorns, bay leaf, and thyme.

Simmer at the lowest heat possible, partially covered, for about 1 1/2 hours, or until the vegetables are completely soft. Strain the stock in three or four batches through a fine sieve with a large bowl underneath. Stock keeps in a sealed container in the refrigerator for about a week, and freezes well.

Pie Crusts—Savory and Sweet

Don't be scared of making your own pastry. It makes a bit of a mess, but it's not that hard, and you can definitely tell the difference between homemade and store-bought. This recipe makes enough for one double-crust pie. You may want to increase the recipe, as the pastry keeps in the refrigerator for up to a week, and it does freeze well in plastic wrap and a resealable bag.

Makes enough pastry for 1 double-crust pie

Basic/Savory Recipe

2 cups	all-purpose flour	500 mL
³/₄ tsp.	salt	4 mL
1 tsp.	baking powder	5 mL
1 cup	vegetable oil shortening	250 mL
1	egg	1
2 Tbsp.	cold water (approx.)	30 mL
1 Tbsp.	white vinegar	15 mL
3 Tbsp.	milk for sealing pastry (approx.)	45 mL

Sift the flour, salt, and baking powder together in a large bowl. Using a pastry blender, two butter knives, or your hands, rub in the shortening until the mixture looks like it has small pebbles in it.

Beat the egg in a small bowl. Add the water and vinegar. Pour into the flour mixture and mix with your hands. Check the consistency. Some of it should be sticking together, but there should be some crumblier bits in the bottom of the bowl—don't expect it to be a large mass, like cookie dough. If you have a mass of dry stuff in the bottom of the bowl, add a little bit more water—you shouldn't add more than an extra 2 Tbsp. (30 mL), and you may need less than that.

Divide the dough in half, pressing each half into a ball. Flatten each ball slightly so it forms a thick patty.

(Continued on next page)

Refrigerating this dough isn't necessary, but if you aren't using it right away, wrap up each patty separately in plastic wrap. Keep in the refrigerator or freezer.

Roll out the first half on a lightly floured surface with a rolling pin. This will be the base. Use your pie plate as a guide—when the dough is about $^3/_4$ inch (2 cm) wider than the outside of the pie plate, it's big enough. Fold the pastry over the rolling pin and carefully lift it into the plate. Press into the plate and trim the outside edge with a pair of scissors—this works much better than a knife.

Roll the second half (the top) out to the same size. After you have filled your pie, place this top layer over the filling, trimming around the outside to match the bottom. Spread a little milk around the edge to help seal the two layers, and flute the edge to make it look pretty. To flute, press the dough with the forefinger of one hand against the wedge made with the finger and thumb of your other hand. If this is too fiddly for you, just press down with your thumb or the tines of a fork to seal the pastry layers.

With a knife, cut several small slits in the top layer of the pastry. Brush lightly with milk before baking.

Sweet Pastry: Make basic/savory pastry, sifting 2 tsp. (10 mL) of sugar in with the flour mixture.

The thing to remember with pastry is that it's not fine china. You can tear it, patch it, mush it up, and start over with no noticeable detriment. That said, here are some pastry survival tips:

- Make sure your counter is floured, but don't heap the flour on there.

- Roll from the center out.

- If you roll out your pastry and it seems to break apart everywhere, take a deep breath, mush it back into a ball, and start rolling all over again.

- If this doesn't work, the pastry is probably too dry. Put it into a bowl and add about a tablespoon (15 mL) of cold water, combine, and start again, making sure to dust well with flour.

- If you roll the pastry out and there are large tears or chasms, figure out the areas that are much larger than they need to be to fit your dish. Cut these off with a knife and trim them to fit the tears. Brush the cracked surface and then "patch" lightly with milk to help it stick. Press together, dust with flour, and roll it out.

- If you don't have a rolling pin, a full wine bottle works well.

- If you are freezing the pie, do it *before* you bake it, and don't cut slits in the top. Cut the slits after it's defrosted, just before you bake it.

breakfasts & brunches

Chocolate Chip and Banana Pancakes

My dad always had a big pitcher of pancake batter in the fridge at his restaurant, and from time to time I'd help him make it. This batter is reminiscent of his own, with my additions of chocolate chips and bananas. I can't forget that morning when I first decided to caramelize the bananas before adding them to the batter—there was just such foodie joy in the air.

Makes about 5 cups (1.25 L) batter, enough for 4-6 people

1 tsp.	butter, plus extra for frying	5 mL
2	ripe bananas, diced	2
2 Tbsp.	brown sugar	30 mL
2 cups	all-purpose flour	500 mL
2 tsp.	baking powder	10 mL
1/2 tsp.	baking soda	2.5 mL
1 tsp.	salt	5 mL
2	eggs	2
2 cups	milk	500 mL
1 1/2 tsp.	vanilla	7.5 mL
1/4 cup	finely chopped semisweet chocolate chips	60 mL

Melt 1 tsp. (5 mL) of butter in a skillet over medium heat. Add the bananas and cook, stirring often, for about a minute. Then add 1 Tbsp. (15 mL) of the brown sugar and stir for 3–4 minutes, or until the bananas look soft and shiny. Transfer to a plate.

In a large bowl, combine the flour, baking powder, baking soda, salt, and the remaining brown sugar. Stir well with a fork to combine, then make a well in the center.

In a small bowl, beat the eggs together. Add the milk and vanilla and stir.

Gradually pour the egg mixture into the well in the center of the flour mixture. Mix together with a fork until the ingredients are incorporated, but don't overmix—some small lumps are okay. Let it sit for about 5 minutes, or until you see a lot of bubbles that have risen to the top of the batter. Stir in the bananas and chocolate chips.

Preheat the oven to 250°F (120°C). Add $^1/_2$ tsp. (2.5 mL) of butter to your skillet over medium-high heat and when the pan is hot, drop in batter by $^1/_4$ cupfuls (60 mL). When lots of bubbles form on the top of the pancakes and the edges are looking like they're starting to cook, turn them over. **Never** turn pancakes over more than once! It can make them tough. When the pancakes are cooked, put them on a cookie sheet in the oven to stay hot. Keep frying pancakes, adding about 1 tsp. (5 mL) of butter for each batch.

Farmer's Blueberry-Oat Pancakes

These pancakes have a nice, rustic taste to them—imagine you're eating them at a charming country inn. The oats add texture, and grinding them makes for a surprisingly light and fluffy pancake. Any berries can be substituted for blueberries here, but if you use strawberries or raspberries, chop them. Grated apple also works well.

Serves 4-6

1 cup	quick-cooking rolled oats	250 mL
1 cup	whole wheat flour	250 mL
1 cup	all-purpose flour	250 mL
2 tsp.	baking powder	10 mL
1/2 tsp.	salt	2.5 mL
1 tsp.	baking soda	5 mL
1/4 cup	white sugar	60 mL
2	eggs	2
2 cups	milk	500 mL
1 Tbsp.	vanilla extract	15 mL
2 cups	blueberries	500 mL
3 Tbsp.	butter (approx.)	45 mL

Spoon the rolled oats into a food processor and blend on high speed until you have a fine powder, about 30 seconds. Combine in a large bowl with the flours, baking powder, salt, soda, and sugar. Form a well in the center and set aside.

In a medium bowl, beat the eggs lightly. Stir in the milk and vanilla to combine.

Pour the egg mixture into the well in the dry ingredients, and stir just until combined—a few lumps are okay. Fold in the berries. This batter is very thick.

Preheat the oven to 250°F (120°C). Melt about 1 tsp. (5 mL) butter over medium-high heat in a large skillet. Spoon the pancake batter into whatever sizes you like. When bubbles start to form on top of the pancake and the bottom has set, flip over. Don't flip pancakes more than once.

Serve with maple syrup and Vanilla Cream Topping (p. 162).

If, like me, you're not really a morning person, combine the dry ingredients for pancakes the night before and keep them in a covered container overnight. This cuts down greatly on the concentration you'll need to put the pancakes together when you're bleary-eyed and grumpy.

To maximize skillet space when making pancakes, pour two larger pancakes opposite each other, and then pour two smaller pancakes opposite each other in the spaces left.

French Toast

This delicious and easy breakfast is a perfect opportunity to use up slightly stale white bread—this can be country bread, challah, whatever, as long as it's not whole wheat and grainy. It can easily be halved for 2–3 people.

Serves 4-6

4	eggs	4
1/4 tsp.	cinnamon, plus extra for sprinkling	1.2 mL
2 Tbsp.	sugar	30 mL
1 cup	milk	250 mL
5 tsp.	butter, for frying (approx.)	25 mL
12 slices	white bread (approx.)	12 slices

Preheat the oven to 200°F (95°C). Beat the eggs for about 1 minute in a large, shallow bowl. Add 1/4 tsp. (1.2 mL) cinnamon and beat in until the cinnamon is well distributed, about 30 seconds. Beat in the sugar, then the milk.

Melt about 1 tsp. (5 mL) butter in a large skillet over medium-high heat. As the butter is melting, dip the bread, 1 or 2 slices at a time, into the egg mixture, flipping over to dip both sides. Transfer to the hot pan and fry for 3–4 minutes on each side, or until golden brown.

Transfer the cooked French toast to a baking sheet in the oven to keep warm as you fry the rest. You may find that your cinnamon has been absorbed by the first few slices of bread; if this is the case, sprinkle a bit on each side of the bread after you've dipped it.

Serve with maple syrup and Vanilla Cream Topping (p. 162).

Cinnamon Peanut Toast

This breakfast treat is quick and easy to prepare, and combines the tastiness of cinnamon toast with a little protein to start your day off right.

Serves 4–6

1/2 cup	natural (unsweetened) peanut butter, smooth or crunchy	125 mL
1/2 cup	brown sugar, packed	125 mL
1/2 tsp.	cinnamon, plus extra for sprinkling	2.5 mL
1/4 tsp.	salt	1.2 mL
2 Tbsp.	milk or soymilk	30 mL
4–6	large slices of bread, whole grain or white	4–6
4 tsp.	butter (approx.)	20 mL

Preheat the oven to 400°F (200°C). In a medium bowl, mix together the peanut butter, sugar, cinnamon, salt, and milk or soymilk. Set aside.

Lightly butter the bread slices and place directly on an oven rack (not on a cookie sheet) for 3–4 minutes, or until the butter is melted and the bread is barely starting to toast.

Remove from the oven and spread a thick layer of peanut topping on each slice. Sprinkle with cinnamon.

Return to the oven for 2–4 minutes, or until the peanut topping is bubbling a bit.

Remove from the oven, cut each slice in half, and serve immediately.

Molasses-Bran Muffins

These humble yet delicious bran muffins were a staple in my parents' restaurant while I was growing up. You may want to double this recipe, as the muffins freeze well in an airtight bag. They're fantastic for breakfast with butter and jam.

Makes 12 muffins

1 1/2 cups	all-purpose flour	375 mL
2 tsp.	baking powder	10 mL
1/2 tsp.	baking soda	2.5 mL
1/2 tsp.	salt	2.5 mL
1 1/2 cups	bran	375 mL
1/2 cup	brown sugar, packed	125 mL
2	eggs	2
1 cup	milk	250 mL
1 tsp.	vanilla	5 mL
1/4 cup	vegetable oil	60 mL
1/4 cup	molasses	60 mL

Preheat the oven to 425°F (220°C). In a large bowl, mix together the flour, baking powder, baking soda, and salt. Set aside.

In a medium bowl, mix together the bran and brown sugar. Set aside.

In a small bowl, beat the eggs lightly. Add the milk and vanilla and stir well. Add the milk mixture to the bran mixture, stirring to combine.

Pour the vegetable oil into a 1/2 cup (125 mL) measuring cup. Top up with molasses. This will make the molasses easier to get out of the cup. Empty the molasses mixture into the bran mixture, using a rubber scraper to get out any last bits of molasses. Stir to combine.

Form a well in the flour mixture. Gradually pour in the bran mixture, stirring in larger and larger circles to incorporate the flour mixture. Stir just until blended—don't overmix.

Grease a 12-muffin pan. Divide the mixture equally among the 12 muffin cups.

Bake for about 12 minutes, or until a knife inserted in the center of a muffin comes out clean. Remove from the oven and run a butter knife around the edges to loosen. Immediately transfer the muffins to a cooling rack, using your knife as a lever to pop the muffins out.

Porridge

This breakfast is humble, yes, but it has an awful lot going for it. First, it's so easy to make that you can actually have it simmering *before* you've made yourself coffee. Second, it doesn't depend on any fresh ingredients at all—perfect when you're out of eggs, yogurt, bread, and other breakfasty foods.

Serves 6

1 1/2 cups	quick-cooking rolled oats	375 mL
1/4 tsp.	salt	1.2 mL
1/2 tsp.	cinnamon	2.5 mL
dash	freshly grated nutmeg	dash
4 cups	water	1 L
	brown sugar, butter, and milk to taste	

Combine the dry ingredients in a medium saucepan. Add the water and bring to a boil over medium-high heat, stirring occasionally at first, and constantly once it starts to thicken. When it starts to bubble, reduce the heat to medium, stirring constantly. Let this bubble for about 3 minutes, or more if you like a thicker porridge.

Serve each bowl with a pat of butter melting on top, as well as about 1/2 tsp. (2.5 mL) of brown sugar per serving. A little milk drizzled over is optional.

Easy Oven Omelette

Omelettes are things that skilled chefs always tell you are easy. Let me clarify: they are easy for the *skilled chefs*.

That's why I came up with this cheater's omelette. It's wonderful, fluffy, and failure-proof. Better yet, It feeds a whole crowd of people—easily!

Serves 4–6

2 tsp.	butter	10 mL
2 cups	sliced mushrooms	500 mL
10	eggs	10
1/4 cup	milk	60 mL
pinch	each salt, pepper, and parsley flakes	pinch
1 cup	grated cheddar	250 mL

Preheat the oven to 350°F (175°C). Melt the butter in a skillet over medium heat. Sauté the mushrooms, stirring occasionally, for 5–6 minutes. Set aside.

In a buttered 8- x 10-inch (20- x 25-cm) dish, break the eggs and beat lightly with a fork until the eggs are uniformly blended, about 30 seconds. Lightly beat in the milk, salt, pepper, parsley, and cheese.

Bake, uncovered, for about 30 minutes, or until the center is cooked. To remove, run a butter knife around the edge of the pan, cut into pieces, and lift out with a spatula or pie server. Serve with toast.

Tofu Scramble

I remember preparing this dish about five years ago while visiting my friend Stephanie in the wilds of northern British Columbia. She thought that the best way to show me the stunning vistas of the region was to go on a daylong hike. With no small amount of griping, I did make it up the mountain, or hill, or whatever it was we climbed that day— thanks, I'm sure, to the generous amount of this dish I had eaten.

Serves 6

1	16-oz. (454-g) package extra-firm tofu, crumbled	1
1 Tbsp.	curry powder	15 mL
1 tsp.	turmeric	5 mL
5 Tbsp.	soy sauce	75 mL
2	cloves garlic, crushed	2
1 Tbsp.	olive oil	15 mL
1	small onion, chopped	1
1 1/2 cups	broccoli florets	375 mL
1	medium carrot, julienned	1
1 1/2 cups	sliced mushrooms	375 mL

In a large bowl, combine the tofu, curry powder, turmeric, 3 Tbsp. (45 mL) soy sauce, and garlic until well mixed. Set aside.

Heat the oil over medium heat in a large, deep skillet. Add the onion, broccoli, and carrot and sauté for about 3 minutes, adding a little water, if necessary, to keep the vegetables moist. Add mushrooms and continue to sauté until vegetables are cooked, adding a little water if you need it, about 5 minutes. Mix in the remaining 2 Tbsp. (30 mL) soy sauce.

Add the tofu mixture and sauté for about 5 minutes, or until the tofu has turned yellow and is heated through.

Serve with toast and ketchup.

Mini Breakfast Quiches

These little quiches are perfect for breakfast, and I've included fillings that are particularly good in the morning—cheese, "bacon," and onions. If you don't have the time to make the individual pastry cups and want to make one big quiche, use the recipe for Cheese and Green Onion Quiche on p. 90.

Serves 4–6

1 batch	Savory Pie Crust (p. 27)	1 batch
1 tsp.	butter	5 mL
1	medium onion, finely chopped	1
2	eggs	2
$^3/_4$ cup	milk	185 mL
$^1/_2$ tsp.	salt	2.5 mL
large pinch	pepper	large pinch
4–5	simulated bacon bits (per quiche)	4–5
1 tsp.	grated old cheddar cheese (per quiche)	5 mL

Preheat the oven to 400°F (200°C). Roll out your pastry dough on a lightly floured surface, half at a time if your surface isn't big enough. Roll out the dough to $^1/_{10}$-inch (.25-cm) thickness. Find a round teacup or bowl about 4 inches (10 cm) in diameter. Cut out 12 rounds.

Place each round into a cup of a 12-muffin pan. Gently shape the dough to the muffin cup, using your fingers to pinch the dough around the top of each cup so the tops have a slightly scalloped appearance.

Find another teacup, glass, or bowl about 3 inches (8 cm) in diameter. Use this to trace 12 circles onto wax or parchment paper. Fold the paper first to shorten the job—make 6 circles on a double thickness or 4 on a triple thickness. Cut out rounds and place one into each pastry cup. Place about $^1/_2$ Tbsp. (7.5 mL) of dried beans in each cup as pie weights.

Bake the cups for 6–7 minutes, or until the tops have turned golden. Remove from the oven and let cool for a few minutes, then carefully remove the paper and beans. Set the pastry cups aside, still in the muffin pan. Turn the oven down to 375°F (190°C).

Melt the butter over medium heat. Add the onion and sauté until browned, about 8 minutes, adding a little water if the onions get too dry. Set aside.

In a medium bowl, beat the eggs for 2–3 minutes, then lightly beat in the milk. Stir in salt and pepper.

Put the onions, "bacon," and cheese in the bottom of each muffin cup, using about 1 tsp. (5 mL) onion for each onion-containing quiche. Fill up with the egg mixture.

Bake for 18–22 minutes, until the filling has puffed up and the centers feel firm when you touch them.

A note on simulated bacon—look for "bacon bits" at the bulk food or grocery store that contain no meat or meat products. Most of them are totally vegetarian. When they're baked into quiche, they become soft and chewy, giving a wonderful smoky flavor and meaty texture. They also expand, so don't overdo it.

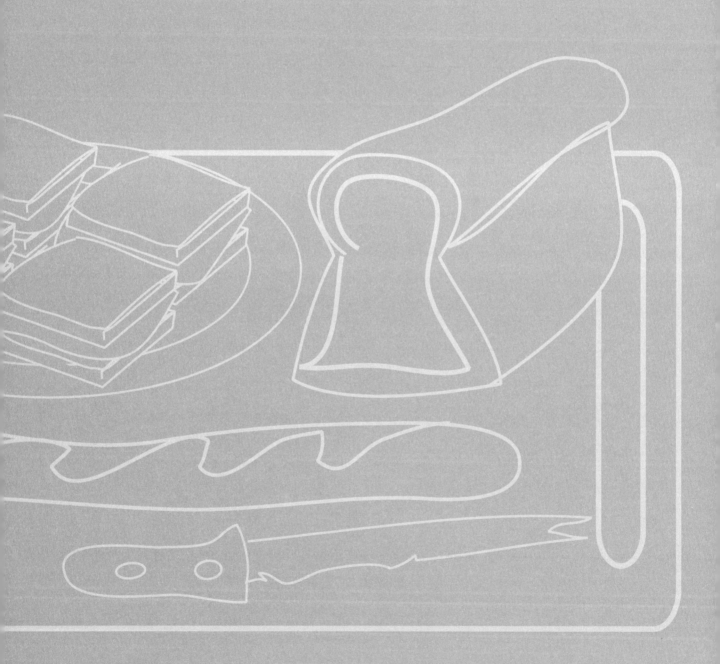

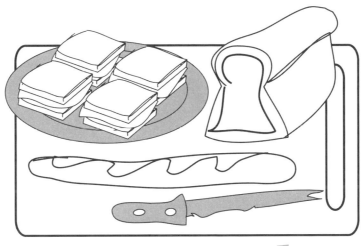

sandwiches

Egg Salad Sandwiches

Here it is, the real thing. An egg salad sandwich is one of the nicest lunches, as far as I'm concerned. You can doll this up with whatever spices you like—curry powder, paprika, dill—but here is the basic recipe that I always start from. It's especially good with tomato and avocado slices on whole grain bread.

Serves 4

6	eggs	6
2 Tbsp.	minced raw onion	30 mL
2 Tbsp.	mayonnaise	30 mL
2 tsp.	Creamy Dressing #2 (p. 75) (optional)	10 mL
pinch	each salt and pepper	pinch

To hard-boil the eggs, use a large spoon to carefully place them in a medium saucepan of gently boiling water. Simmer them gently for about 10 minutes. Run the eggs under cold water for a few seconds to cool them enough to handle. Break the shells by tapping each egg on the counter and then pulling the crushed shells off with your fingers under cold running water—they will come off easily.

Pat eggs dry with a paper towel. Finely chop the eggs and put them into a medium bowl. Add the rest of the ingredients and mix together. Add more salt or pepper to taste.

Avocado-Tomato Melt

This sandwich is a homemade version of uppity vegetarian melts I've had in restaurants. This one's better.

Serves 4-6

2	small cloves garlic, crushed	2
2 Tbsp.+ 1/4 cup	mayonnaise	90 mL
1 tsp.	fresh rosemary	5 mL
2	foot-long (30 cm) baguettes	2
2	ripe avocados, sliced	2
2	tomatoes, sliced	2
	salt and pepper to taste	
1 cup	cheddar, swiss, or havarti cheese, thinly sliced	250 mL

Preheat the oven to 375°F (190°C). In a small bowl, combine the garlic, mayonnaise, and rosemary. Set aside.

Cut each baguette in half lengthwise, then in half crosswise, so that you have eight 6-inch (15-cm) slices. Spread baguette slices on a cookie sheet. Spread 1 tsp. (5 mL) of the mayonnaise mixture onto each slice. Top this with a layer of avocado, then a layer of tomato.

Sprinkle with salt and pepper and top with a layer of cheese.

Bake, uncovered, for 10–12 minutes, or until the cheese is bubbling and browned in spots. Let sit for 2–3 minutes, then serve.

Fried 'Nanner Sandwiches

Elvis Presley reportedly loved these sandwiches, which should be more than enough reason for you to try them. Add to this that they're full of protein and the bananas caramelize in the sandwich in a heavenly way, and you should be getting your peanut butter out by now.

Serves 4

¹/₃ cup	natural (unsweetened) peanut butter, smooth or crunchy	80 mL
¹/₄ cup	firmly packed brown sugar	60 mL
pinch	salt	pinch
2	large bananas, peeled and chopped	2
2–3 Tbsp.	milk or soymilk	30–45 mL
8	large slices of bread, white or whole grain	8
¹/₄ cup	butter (approx.)	60 mL

In a medium bowl, mix together the peanut butter, sugar, and salt until thoroughly combined. Add the bananas, then mix in enough milk or soymilk to creat a soft, spreadable consistency.

Spread one side of each slice of bread with butter. Take one slice of buttered bread and spread a thick layer of filling on the *unbuttered* side. Place another slice of buttered bread on top, with the buttered side facing up, so you have a sandwich whose outsides are buttered. Continue with the rest of the bread slices.

Melt about 1 Tbsp. (15 mL) butter in a large skillet over medium heat. When the butter is hot, add as many sandwiches as will fit. Fry on each side for 3–5 minutes, or until golden brown, pressing down with your pancake flipper once or twice to speed the process.

Add more butter to the pan for each round of sandwiches. Cut each sandwich in half before serving.

Grilled Cheese Sandwiches

The trick to a good grilled cheese sandwich is pressing the sandwich as it cooks. This melts the cheese without burning the bread, and holds the sandwich together. For those of us who don't have a sandwich-maker, an equally effective alternative is to use the old-fashioned method of a saucer and weights. If you've got a bit of extra time, try the variation—it's fantastic.

Serves 4

8 slices	white or whole grain bread	8 slices
2–3 Tbsp.	butter	30–45 mL
8–12 slices	cheddar cheese	8–12 slices

Generously butter one side of each bread slice. For each sandwich, place 2–3 slices of cheese on the **unbuttered** side of the first slice, then cover with a second slice, buttered side out.

Melt about $^1/_2$ tsp. (2.5 mL) butter per sandwich in a skillet over medium heat. Carefully place as many sandwiches as will fit in the pan. Rest a saucer (or plate) over the sandwiches, then weigh it down with kitchen weights or something similarly heavy. (Do not allow the saucer to touch the hot pan.) Cook 5–7 minutes on each side, until the bread turns golden brown and the cheese has melted. (Take care when removing the saucer, as it may be hot.)

Slice the sandwiches in half and serve with ketchup. For a deli-style lunch, accompany with Colorful Coleslaw (p. 66) and a sliced dill pickle.

Grilled Onion and Cheese Sandwiches: Sauté half a finely sliced onion per sandwich in a skillet with $^1/_4$ tsp. (2.5 mL) butter over medium heat until soft and slightly browned. When putting together the sandwich, top the cheese with a layer of the sautéed onions. Fry as directed above.

Welsh Rarebit

This is sometimes called "Welsh Rabbit," and I've always wondered why. Was it for the poor Welsh who could not afford rabbit, or was it for the discerning vegetarian Welsh? I have heard two theories. One takes apart the word "rarebit"; it's literally a lightly cooked (rare) snack (bit). The other involves the old carnivore sob story: this was the snack for those who could not find a rabbit to eat. Either way, make sure you raise a toast with the leftover beer after making this delicious cheese sauce, to the cute little rabbit you are not eating.

Serves 4

1	egg	1
1 cup	milk	250 mL
2 Tbsp.	butter	30 mL
1 Tbsp.	flour	15 mL
1/2 cup	beer, flat if possible	125 mL
1 tsp.	Dijon mustard	5 mL
1/4 tsp.	paprika	1.2 mL
dash	cayenne	dash
1 1/2 cups	medium or old cheddar cheese, grated	375 mL
	4 large slices of whole grain bread, or 8 small slices of whole grain bread	
2	medium tomatoes, thinly sliced	2
	salt and pepper to taste	

In a small bowl, beat the egg, and then add the milk. Set aside. Melt the butter in a small to medium saucepan over medium heat. Add the flour to form a roux. Add the beer, whisking constantly. If your beer is not flat, it will fizz up, but don't worry about it. Still whisking, add the mustard, paprika, and cayenne. Continue to heat, whisking constantly, until the sauce starts to thicken, 3–4 minutes.

Add the cheddar and whisk until the cheese is melted, about a minute. Add 2–3 Tbsp. (30–45 mL) of the hot cheese mixture to the egg mixture and whisk together in the bowl. Gradually add the milk mixture to the cheese mixture in the saucepan, whisking constantly to incorporate it. Then, once it's smooth, heat at medium until the sauce starts to thicken and bubble, stirring occasionally. Add salt to taste.

On a baking sheet, arrange the bread slices and put a layer of sliced tomatoes on each piece. Heat under the broiler for about 5 minutes, or until the tomatoes are heated through but not burning.

Arrange the bread on plates and pour cheese sauce over top. Top with freshly ground black pepper.

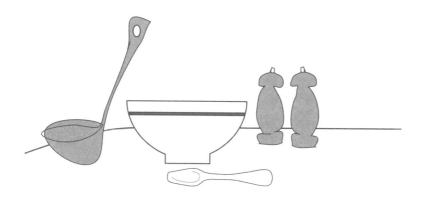

soups

Cream of Mushroom Soup

Erase all thoughts of junky canned soup from your memory, and replace them with this elegant, velvety soup. Feel free to substitute the sliced cap of one large portobello mushroom for 1 cup (250 mL) of white button mushrooms—this gives the soup a richer, more earthy flavor. And if you're feeling really decadent, use cream instead of milk.

Serves 4–6

1 Tbsp.	butter	15 mL
2	stalks celery, finely chopped	2
1	medium onion, finely chopped	1
2	bay leaves	2
4 cups	sliced mushrooms	1 L
5 cups	vegetable stock	1.25 L
1/2 tsp.	salt	2.5 mL
1/2 tsp.	dried savory	2.5 mL
1 Tbsp.	flour	15 mL
3/4 cup	milk	185 mL
1/4 tsp.	white or black pepper	1.2 mL

Melt the butter in a large saucepan over medium heat. Add the celery and onion and sauté, stirring occasionally, for about 5 minutes or until the onions are slightly softened. Add the bay leaves, mushrooms, 1/2 cup (125 mL) stock, salt, and savory. Stir well, reduce the heat to medium-low, and cover. Simmer for 5–7 minutes, stirring occasionally. Uncover and add the flour, stirring to coat.

Add the rest of the stock, stir well, and raise the heat to bring it to a boil, stirring occasionally. Reduce the heat and simmer, partially covered, for 20–25 minutes. Remove the bay leaves and set aside about 1/2 cup (125 mL) sliced mushrooms. Transfer the soup to a blender and blend on high speed until smooth.

Return the soup to the pot over medium heat. Add the reserved sliced mushrooms, the milk and pepper, and heat through.

Cauliflower and Corn Chowder

When you're in the mood for a creamy, hearty soup, this one will fit the bill—without the use of milk or cream. This soup makes a filling meal with bread and salad.

Serves 6

1 Tbsp.	butter	15 mL
2	medium onions, finely chopped	2
3	large cloves garlic, finely chopped	3
1	medium cauliflower, cut into small florets (about 5 cups/1.25 L)	1
1	medium potato, peeled and chopped	1
5 cups	vegetable stock	1.25 L
1	12-oz. (341-mL) can corn kernels with liquid	1
1	bay leaf	1
3/4 tsp.	salt	4 mL
1/2 tsp.	dried sage	2.5 mL
large pinch	white pepper	large pinch

Melt the butter in a large saucepan over medium heat. Add the onions and garlic and sauté for about 5 minutes. Add the cauliflower, potato, and 1/4 cup (60 mL) stock and continue to sauté for another 6–8 minutes.

Add the corn kernels with liquid, bay leaf, salt, and sage, and sauté for about 2 minutes. Add the remaining stock and simmer partially covered, stirring occasionally, for 15–20 minutes or until the potatoes and cauliflower have softened.

Put about half the soup into a blender, making sure to leave lots of vegetable chunks in the pot, and blend until completely smooth, 1–2 minutes. Return the blended soup to the saucepan and stir to combine. Simmer for another 5 minutes or so, and check consistency. If it's too chunky for your taste, blend a bit more. Add pepper. Serve.

Cream of Tomato Soup

This delicious soup really does honor its unassuming roots, yet it tastes so much better than the prefab cornstarchy stuff.

Serves 6

2	28-oz. (796-mL) cans tomatoes, whole or diced	2
2 Tbsp.	butter	30 mL
1	medium onion, chopped	1
1	stalk celery, finely chopped	1
2	cloves garlic, finely chopped	2
1 tsp.	dried basil	5 mL
1/2 tsp.	dried oregano	2.5 mL
1/4 tsp.	dried thyme	1.2 mL
3 Tbsp.	flour	45 mL
1 1/4 tsp.	salt	6.2 mL
1 Tbsp.	honey	15 mL
3 cups	vegetable stock	750 mL
1 1/2 cups	milk	375 mL
	freshly ground black pepper	

If you're using whole tomatoes, empty them into a large bowl with their liquid, and use a potato masher to mash them into smaller pieces. Set aside.

Melt the butter in a large saucepan over medium heat. Add the onion, celery, and garlic and sauté, stirring often, for 4–5 minutes, then add the basil, oregano, and thyme and sauté for another 2–3 minutes, or until the vegetables have softened and browned slightly.

Add the flour and stir to coat the vegetables. Cook for about 1 minute, stirring constantly. Add the tomatoes, with liquid, and bring to a simmer. Simmer gently, partially covered, for about 5 minutes. Stir in the salt and honey.

Add the stock and simmer, uncovered, for about 20 minutes, until the soup has thickened and reduced. Transfer the soup to a food processor or blender and purée until smooth—you will have to do this in at least two batches.

Return the soup to the saucepan and bring to a gentle simmer. Stir in the milk and simmer for 3–4 minutes. Either stir in a generous amount of black pepper before serving, or grind black pepper onto individual portions if desired.

Minestrone

"Minestra" is Italian for soup; "minestrone" is Italian for big soup. This version lives up to its name, as it makes an excellent main course with some crusty bread. It also makes a great starter that will please a large, meat-eating family—I know from experience.

Serves 4–6

1 Tbsp.	olive oil	15 mL
1	large red or yellow onion, finely chopped	1
1	large carrot, peeled and finely chopped	1
3	stalks celery, finely chopped	3
4	cloves garlic, minced	4
5 cups	vegetable stock	1.25 L
1 1/2 cups	green cabbage, chopped into 1/2-inch (1-cm) squares	375 mL
1/2 tsp.	salt	2.5 mL
1 tsp.	basil	5 mL
1 tsp.	oregano	5 mL
1	28-oz. (796-mL) can tomatoes with their liquid	1
1/2	19-oz. (540-mL) can chickpeas, drained and rinsed	1/2
1/4 cup	red wine	60 mL
1/4 tsp.	black pepper	1.2 mL
1/2 bunch	fresh parsley, finely chopped	1/2 bunch
1/3 cup	romano or parmesan cheese (optional) (approx.)	80 mL

Heat the oil over medium heat in a large saucepan. Add the onion, carrot, celery, and garlic and sauté, stirring often, for about 5 minutes, adding a little stock if the vegetables stick. Add the cabbage, 1/2 cup (125 mL) stock, salt, basil, and oregano, and simmer, partially covered, for 5 minutes. Break up the tomatoes into the soup with your hands. Stir in the tomato liquid from the can, then add the chickpeas and remaining stock.

Simmer, partially covered, for 30 minutes, or until the vegetables are tender. Add wine and simmer, partially covered, for 10 minutes more. Add pepper just before serving.

Ladle into bowls and garnish with fresh parsley and cheese, if desired.

Curried Squash Soup

This soup is uncomplicated, but the earthy squash and curry seasonings make for a rich, elegant flavor. Beautiful with a dollop of sour cream or yogurt floating on top.

Serves 6

1 Tbsp.	butter	15 mL
2	large onions, finely chopped	2
4	cloves garlic, minced	4
1	medium carrot, peeled and finely chopped	1
2 tsp.	curry powder	10 mL
1 tsp.	cumin	5 mL
1	large butternut squash, peeled, seeded and chopped (about 6 cups/1.5 mL)	1
1	bay leaf	1
1 tsp.	salt	5 mL
6 cups	vegetable stock	1.5 L
	sour cream or yogurt for garnish	

Melt the butter in a large saucepan over medium heat. Add the onions, garlic, and carrot, and sauté for 5 minutes, adding a little stock if onions start to brown.

Stir in the curry powder and cumin, and sauté, stirring constantly, for about 2 minutes. Add the squash, bay leaf, salt, and 1 cup (250 mL) of stock. Simmer, partially covered, stirring occasionally, for about 15 minutes, or until the squash is completely soft.

Add the remaining stock and simmer gently, partially covered, for 25 minutes. Remove the bay leaf and transfer the soup to a food processor or blender—you will need to do this in two batches so as not to make a mess. Purée until completely smooth.

Serve with a dollop of sour cream or yogurt in the center of each portion.

Sweet Potato-Lentil Soup

Perfect for the dead of winter, when more exotic vegetables can be difficult to find. The ample helping of sautéed onions and leeks makes complex seasoning unnecessary in this subtly sweet soup.

Serves 6

1¹/₂ cups	dried red lentils, rinsed well	375 mL
3	medium onions, chopped	3
3	carrots, peeled and chopped	3
2	leeks, greens removed and whites chopped	2
2 Tbsp.	olive oil	30 mL
1 Tbsp.	butter	15 mL
2 tsp.	salt	10 mL
2	medium sweet potatoes, peeled and chopped	2
1 tsp.	powdered sage	5 mL
2	bay leaves	2
6 cups	vegetable stock	1.5 L
1 tsp.	Marmite, dissolved in 1 cup (250 mL) warm water	5 mL

Put the rinsed lentils in a large bowl, covering with at least 4 inches (10 cm) of cold water. Let stand for 1 hour. While the lentils are soaking, peel and chop the vegetables.

In a large pot, sauté the onions, carrots, and leeks in oil and butter on medium heat for 8–10 minutes, adding 1 tsp. (5 mL) of salt during cooking. Add the sweet potatoes and sauté for 3–4 minutes. Drain the lentils and add to the pot with the sage and bay leaves, stirring thoroughly.

Add the stock, Marmite solution, and remaining teaspoon (5 mL) of salt. Simmer partially covered, stirring occasionally, for 45–60 minutes, or until the sweet potatoes and carrots are soft. Serve as is or, for a heartier texture, transfer half the soup to a blender or food processor, purée until smooth, and return to the pot.

Split Pea Soup

This soup is rich and satisfying, cheap, and extremely good for you. To re-enact the Canadian, men's-men-type heritage of this soup, sprinkle simulated bacon bits on each portion just before serving. How rugged!

Serves 6

1 1/2 cups	dried split green peas	375 mL
1 Tbsp.	olive oil	15 mL
2	medium-large onions, finely chopped	2
1	large carrot, peeled and finely chopped	1
3	cloves garlic, minced	3
1 tsp.	dried sage	5 mL
1/2 tsp.	dried savory	2.5 mL
3/4 tsp.	salt	4 mL
6 cups	vegetable stock	1.5 L
large pinch	black pepper	large pinch

Pick out any discolored peas from the bunch. Rinse the peas well under cold running water. Transfer to a medium bowl and cover with at least 3 inches (8 cm) of cold water. Let soak for about 2 hours.

In a large saucepan, heat the olive oil over medium heat. Add the onions, carrot, and garlic, and sauté, stirring often, for 5–7 minutes.

Drain the peas. Reduce the heat to medium-low and add the peas, sage, savory, salt, and 1 cup (250 mL) stock. Simmer, partially covered, for about 5 minutes.

Add the rest of the stock and continue to simmer, partially covered, for about 40 minutes or until the peas are soft.

Transfer the soup to a food processor or blender and purée until smooth. Return to the pot, add pepper, and serve hot.

Vegetable Barley Soup

While I was writing this cookbook, my boss Greg called asking for a barley soup recipe to make for his wife Anne, who was sick at home. I didn't have one so I made one up that is full of garlic and vegetables and the things that will keep your strength up. Feel free to experiment with vegetables here—if you don't have parsnips, use rutabaga or more carrots instead.

Serves 6–8

1 Tbsp.	olive oil	15 mL
2	large onions, chopped	2
4	large cloves garlic, finely chopped	4
6 cups	vegetable stock	1.5 L
2	large carrots, peeled and chopped	2
2	large stalks celery, chopped	2
2	parsnips, peeled and chopped	2
1	bay leaf	1
1 tsp.	salt	5 mL
1 tsp.	savory	5 mL
1/3 cup	pearl barley, rinsed	80 mL
1/4 tsp.	pepper	1.2 mL

Heat the olive oil in a large saucepan over medium heat. Add the onions and garlic and sauté for 5–7 minutes or until softened, adding about 1/4 cup (60 mL) stock halfway through.

Add the carrots, celery, parsnip, bay leaf, 1/2 tsp. (2.5 mL) of salt, savory, barley, and 1/2 cup (125 mL) stock. Simmer, partially covered, stirring occasionally, for about 10 minutes.

Add the remaining stock and salt. Simmer partially covered, stirring occasionally, for 35–40 minutes or until the barley and vegetables are soft.

Remove the bay leaf and stir in the pepper. Serve as is, or purée 1/3–1/2 of the soup and return it to the pot.

French Onion Soup

This is my absolute favorite soup for a party or special dinner. It's simple to make, yet it tastes extremely rich and complex. You just need patience: it's crucial that you let the onions caramelize fully until they're brown—this gives the broth its mellow taste and dark color. You can make the broth a day ahead and simply reheat it when you're ready to serve.

Serves 4–6

1/4 cup	butter	60 mL
6	large onions, thinly sliced	6
1/2–3/4 tsp.	salt	2.5–4 mL
1/4 tsp.	sugar	1.2 mL
1/2 cup	white wine	125 mL
2 Tbsp.	soy sauce	30 mL
2 Tbsp.	all-purpose flour	30 mL
6 cups	vegetable stock	1.5 L
1/4 tsp.	black pepper	1.2 mL
8–12	1-inch (2.5-cm) slices of baguette	8–12
4–6	large slices gruyère cheese	4–6

Melt the butter over medium heat in a large, heavy saucepan. Add the onions, 1/4 tsp. (1.2 mL) salt, and sugar, and sauté until the onions have softened and reduced, 10–15 minutes.

Cover, reduce the heat to medium-low, and continue to cook the onions, stirring occasionally, for another 20–25 minutes, or until they have become extremely soft and mushy and have produced liquid.

Remove the cover, increase the heat to medium, and sauté for another 10–15 minutes, or until the onions are evenly browned. Stir in the wine and soy sauce and simmer until reduced to a glaze, about 3 minutes. Stir in the flour thoroughly and let cook for about 1 minute. Add the stock, bring to a boil, and simmer, partially covered, for 20 minutes. Add pepper and remaining salt to taste.

Toast the baguette slices lightly. Fill each soup bowl $^2/_3$–$^3/_4$ full of soup, then wedge 2 baguette slices side by side on top of the soup—you may need to squeeze the slices first so you can fit them in more easily. Top each bowl with 1 slice of gruyère.

Arrange your oven racks—one on the highest rung and one on the lowest. Put a baking sheet on the lowest rack, because the cheese will drip. Set the bowls on the upper rack, under the broiler, for 4–6 minutes, until the cheese is bubbling and slightly browned. Serve immediately—provide people with knives to cut through the bread.

Keep an eye out at garage sales or thrift stores for French onion soup bowls—they're the heavy earthenware ones with the long rodlike handles. Or ask your relatives. They may have some hidden in the "antiquities section" of the basement.

salads

Colorful Coleslaw

Here's a great way to impress people at your next picnic, potluck, or Super Bowl party. Almost no one makes their own coleslaw, yet it's quite simple to make yourself. This version is the real classic that you would find in any good, self-respecting deli. Do make this well in advance—it needs at least 6 hours to marinate, and tastes even better after a day or two.

Serves 6

¹/₂ cup	white vinegar	125 mL
¹/₄ cup	granulated sugar	60 mL
1 tsp.	salt	5 mL
¹/₄ tsp.	mustard powder	1.2 mL
¹/₄ tsp.	black pepper	1.2 mL
dash	paprika	dash
5 cups	finely shredded green cabbage	1.25 L
1 cup	finely shredded red cabbage	250 mL
1	small carrot, peeled and grated	1
1 Tbsp.	onion, grated	15 mL

To make the dressing, combine the vinegar, sugar, salt, mustard, pepper, and paprika in a small saucepan. Heat to boiling, whisking often. Let boil for a minute or so, then remove from heat. Let cool slightly.

Toss the green and red cabbage, carrot, and onion together in a large bowl or plastic container with a sealable lid. Pour the dressing over; it should be slightly warm. Toss thoroughly to coat.

Cover and chill in the refrigerator, tossing every hour or so, for at least 6 hours. A day or more of marinating is preferable—just toss it whenever you remember to.

Avocado with Creamy Dressing

When I was growing up, my dad would occasionally serve a very delicious starter rather than the usual soup or salad: a halved ripe avocado still in the peel, with a generous dollop of mayonnaise where the pit used to be. I still love avocados this way—rich and definitely not low-fat.

Serves 4

2	ripe avocados	2
1/4–1/3 cup	Creamy Dressing #2 (p. 75)	60–80 mL
	coarsely ground black pepper	

Cut the avocados in half lengthwise and remove the pit carefully.

Put the halved avocados in four small, shallow bowls. Spoon about 1 Tbsp. (15 mL) dressing into the center of each. Top with a few grinds of fresh pepper, and serve immediately.

Creamy Vegetable-Chickpea Salad

This salad makes a great lunch on its own, and is also a fantastic filling for pitas. The creamy dressing makes it taste nostalgically like a chicken or tuna salad sandwich—in a good way!

Serves 4

2	large stalks celery, diced	2
1	carrot, peeled and diced	1
1	tomato, chopped	1
1 cup	chickpeas, rinsed and drained	250 mL
$1/4$ cup	finely chopped red onion	60 mL
$1/4$ cup + 2 Tbsp.	Creamy Dressing #2 (p. 75)	90 mL
large pinch	each salt and pepper	large pinch

Combine the vegetables in a large bowl, and toss with dressing, salt and pepper.

Three-Color Cucumber Salad

This is a cheerful, simple salad to serve on the side of a lunch or dinner, and it's very cooling in the summertime.

Serves 4

1	large English cucumber, 12–14 inches (30–38 cm)	1
7	radishes, thinly sliced	7
1	large carrot, peeled and thinly sliced	1
1/8 cup	very finely sliced red onion	30 mL
1/4 cup + 1 Tbsp.	Creamy Dressing #1 (p. 75)	75 mL
large pinch	pepper	large pinch

Rinse and dry the cucumber. Cut the ends off, then drag a fork lengthwise down the cucumber to score the skin. Rotate the cucumber and continue to score until you've done the whole surface. Rinse and dry the cucumber again. Slice the cucumber into 1/8-inch (.3-cm) rounds.

Put the cucumber and radish slices into a salad spinner and dry them, or pat them dry between two paper towels or clean tea towels.

In a large bowl or plastic container with a tight-fitting lid, combine the cucumber, radish, carrot, and onion. Toss with dressing and pepper.

Chill for about 30 minutes before serving. Toss again and serve.

Summertime Salad Platter

I've given this, one of my very favorite starters, its name not because you can only make it in the summertime, but because the tomatoes are nicest and the sweet, mild Vidalia onions are most plentiful then. This is a beautiful and delicious salad to serve with a special dinner.

Serves 4-6

1/2	large Vidalia onion, peeled and thinly sliced	1/2
3	large tomatoes, thinly sliced	3
2	ripe avocados, peeled, pitted, and thinly sliced	2
1/4-1/3 cup	Maple Syrup Vinaigrette (p. 74)	60-80 mL
	salt and freshly ground black pepper	

If you have a very large circular platter (at least 12 inches (30 cm) in diameter), use that. Otherwise, assemble the salad on individual dinner plates.

Separate the onion slices into rings—you don't have to separate them all into individual rings, but make sure you don't serve any whole slices.

Arrange slices of tomato, avocado, and onion in a circular alternating pattern on the plate(s). The easiest way to do this is to start with loosely arranged tomato slices—with a bit of space between slices. Tuck onion slices over and under the tomatoes, so that they're overlapping, and then do the same with the avocado. You will have overlapping slices of everything arranged almost like a circular tart.

Drizzle dressing evenly over the salad. Let sit for a couple of minutes, but no more than 5. Grind black pepper generously over top and sprinkle with a bit of salt. Serve immediately.

Prepare the avocados right before you're ready to serve the salad—otherwise they'll discolor.

Potato Salad

I have yet to meet anyone who doesn't like potato salad. This versatile dish can go from picnic to potluck to just about anywhere, with just about anything. If it's summer and you're feeling nostalgic, whip up a batch of lemonade (p.115) to go with it.

Serves 4–6

4	large boiling potatoes with thin skins, scrubbed, with eyes and blemishes removed	4
$^1/_3$ cup	mayonnaise	80 mL
2 Tbsp.	yogurt	30 mL
2 Tbsp.	fresh chopped dill	30 mL
$^1/_2$ tsp.	garlic powder	2.5 mL
$^1/_2$ tsp.	salt	2.5 mL
large pinch	black pepper	large pinch
$^1/_4$ cup	finely chopped red onion	60 mL
2	stalks celery, finely chopped	2

Cut the potatoes into 1-inch (2.5-cm) cubes and cover with water in a large saucepan. Boil gently for 20–25 minutes, or until they are thoroughly cooked but not mushy. Drain the potatoes and let them cool.

In a large bowl, mix together the mayonnaise, yogurt, dill, garlic powder, salt, and pepper. Add the potatoes, onion, and celery, and toss in the dressing until well mixed.

Cover and chill for at least $^1/_2$ hour before serving.

Warm Mushroom Salad

This is an extremely elegant first course or side dish for a special meal. The recipe calls for regular white button mushrooms, but do feel free to substitute with portobellos, oysters, criminis, or a mixture. Note: The quality of this salad will depend on the quality of your olive oil, as well as that of your wine. No plonk that's gone off!

Serves 4–6

1/2 cup	olive oil	125 mL
6	cloves garlic, sliced	6
6 cups	sliced mushrooms	1.5 L
1/3 cup + 2 tsp.	red wine	90 mL
2 Tbsp.	balsamic vinegar	30 mL
1/2 tsp.	salt	2.5 mL
1/2 tsp.	pepper	2.5 mL
6 cups	exotic mixed greens, curly red or green lettuce, or a combination, washed, dried, and torn	1.5 L

Heat the oil in a large, deep skillet over medium heat. Sauté the garlic in oil for about a minute, or until you can smell a rich garlic aroma. Add the mushrooms and sauté for about 5 minutes, or until the mushrooms have softened and released some liquid. Add the wine and simmer, stirring occasionally, for 2–3 minutes. Add the vinegar, salt, and pepper, and simmer for 3–4 minutes.

Divide the greens into equal portions on as many plates as you have guests, or empty all the greens into a large shallow bowl. Spoon the mushrooms over the greens and drizzle the warm wine dressing over top. Serve immediately.

dressings,
dips & sauces

Maple Syrup Vinaigrette

The inspiration for this vinaigrette comes from my sister Lesley, who made a version of it years ago that I remodelled to my own tastes. It's got a sweet, garlicky, tangy taste, and your guests will compliment you on it. As with all salad dressings, the better the quality of olive oil and vinegar you use, the better it will taste.

Serves 4-6

1/2 cup	olive oil	125 mL
1/4 cup	balsamic vinegar	60 mL
2 Tbsp.	maple syrup	30 mL
1/2 tsp.	salt	2.5 mL
1/4 tsp.	pepper	1.2 mL
1/2 tsp.	dried basil leaves	2.5 mL
2	small cloves garlic, crushed	2

Put all ingredients into a jam jar, plastic container with a tight-fitting lid, or blender/food processor. Shake or blend on low speed until the ingredients are combined.

If you are in the habit of making your own vinaigrettes rather than using the bottled stuff, don't throw out your jam jars. They are fantastic for making salad dressings, as they have a wide enough mouth to easily fit all of your ingredients. They also have a tight screw-top lid so that you don't splatter the stuff all over the kitchen. Just pour into an elegant little jug before serving.

Creamy Dressing #1

This dressing is light and zesty, and makes a perfect Caesar salad. It's also used for Three-Color Cucumber Salad (p. 68). The thickness of this dressing will depend on the yogurt you're using—if it's too thick, blend in water by the tablespoon (15 mL) until you reach a consistency you like. Both this dressing and Creamy Dressing #2 take minutes to whip up in the food processor.

Makes about 1¼ cups (300 mL) dressing

1 cup	plain yogurt	250 mL
1	very small clove garlic, coarsely chopped	1
2 Tbsp.	olive oil	30 mL
2 heaping Tbsp.	fresh parsley, chopped	35–40 mL
½ tsp.	salt	2.5 mL

Put all ingredients into a food processor and process until smooth, about 1 minute, scraping down the sides of the processor halfway through.

Creamy Dressing #2

This mayonnaise-based dressing lends whatever it touches a very '50s diner kind of taste. It's fantastic as a dressing for egg salad, and tastes great in sandwiches and pitas with whatever fillings you like. As with Creamy Dressing #1, add more water in small increments, if necessary, until you reach a consistency you like.

Makes about ¾ cup (185 mL) dressing

¼ cup + 1 Tbsp.	light mayonnaise	75 mL
3 Tbsp.	plain yogurt	45 mL
3 Tbsp.	water	45 mL
4	miniature sweet pickled onions, coarsely chopped	4
1 tsp.	honey	5 mL
1 tsp.	chopped fresh parsley	5 mL
¼ tsp.	salt	1.2 mL
large pinch	mustard powder	large pinch

Put all ingredients into a food processor and process until smooth, about 1 minute, scraping down the sides of the processor halfway through.

Asian Sesame Salad Dressing

This recipe is a homage to a wonderful little pan-Asian eatery in Toronto, the Don Don Noodle Café, where I often used to go. The proprietor made his own salad dressing, and it was so good that doctors and nurses from a nearby hospital would ask him for bottles of the stuff. I was too shy to ask him his secret, but I think this dressing is a competitor!

Makes ¾ cup (185 mL) dressing

1 Tbsp.	sesame seeds	15 mL
¼ cup + 1 Tbsp.	peanut oil	75 mL
1 Tbsp.	rice vinegar	15 mL
1	small clove garlic, chopped coarsely	1
1 Tbsp.	soy sauce	15 mL
2 Tbsp.	water	30 mL
1 Tbsp.	sesame oil	15 mL
2 tsp.	Indonesian Soy Sauce (Ketjap Manis) (p. 78), or 1 tsp. (5 mL) soy sauce and 1 tsp. (5 mL) molasses	10 mL

Preheat the oven to 375°F (190°C). Toast the sesame seeds on a small baking sheet in the oven for about 5 minutes, or until you can smell a rich sesame aroma. Let cool slightly.

Put all ingredients into a blender or food processor, including the sesame seeds. Purée on high speed until the sesame seeds have broken into smaller pieces, 1–2 minutes.

Guacamole

This version of guacamole is a great deal simpler than most other recipes—I find avocados so blissful that I don't like to tart them up too much. And I think you will agree. I've had several people tell me that this is the best guacamole they've ever tasted. Enjoy it as part of a Mexican dinner, on its own as a dip, or spread on toast.

Serves 4

2	very ripe avocados, chopped	2
¼ tsp.	chili powder	1.2 mL
¼ tsp.	salt	1.2 mL
1	small clove garlic, crushed	1
1	ripe tomato, chopped (optional)	1

Use a fork to mash the avocados in a small bowl until smooth—a few chunks are all right. Mix in chili powder, salt, and garlic. Add chopped tomato, if using, and serve immediately.

Avocados turn black very quickly after they're exposed to air. If you're not serving this dip right away, or if you need to store leftovers, empty into a narrow drinking glass or a fairly narrow jar. Smooth out so that the top is even and squeeze a layer of lime juice over top. This will keep the dip from discoloring. Cover with plastic wrap. When you're ready to use it, just stir the lime juice in or pour it off.

Hummus

This hummus is very simple and it always gets compliments. The trick is to use water, rather than a lot of oil, to liquify the dip—this keeps it from becoming too heavy. Use it as a dip or a spread on sandwiches, or spread a layer onto your plate before heaping a vegetable stir-fry, like Spicy Soy Stir-Fry (p. 87), on top.

Makes about 2 cups (500 mL)

1 1/2 cups	canned chickpeas, drained and rinsed	375 mL
2 tsp.	tahini	10 mL
2 tsp.	olive oil	10 mL
1	clove garlic, roughly chopped	1
1/4 tsp.	salt	1.2 mL
large pinch	pepper	large pinch
1/2 tsp.	lemon juice	2.5 mL
1/4 cup	cold water	60 mL

Put all ingredients into a food processor and process on high speed until smooth (about 2 minutes), stopping it a couple of times to scrape down the sides. Serve.

Extra hummus keeps refrigerated in an airtight container for 4–5 days.

Indonesian Soy Sauce (Ketjap Manis)

This sweet, rich soy sauce is a great condiment to use in Asian dishes. It makes a wonderful glaze, and it also plays a supporting role in Peanut Sauce (p. 79).

Makes about 1/2 cup (125 mL)

1/4 cup	brown sugar, packed	60 mL
2 Tbsp.	molasses	30 mL
3 Tbsp.	soy sauce	45 mL
2 Tbsp.	water	30 mL

Combine all ingredients in a small saucepan. Slowly bring to a boil over medium heat, stirring often. When the sauce comes to a boil, reduce the heat and simmer very gently, stirring constantly, for about 3 minutes, or until the sauce starts to thicken. Remove from heat and let cool.

Extra sauce can be refrigerated in a sealed container for 5–7 days.

Peanut Sauce

Once I have peanut sauce around, I start to find dishes to use it in, like Skewer-Free Vegetable Satay (p. 86), or as a dip for Egg Rolls (p.148). This one is silky, zesty, and rich. Enjoy sparingly.

Makes about 1 cup (250 mL)

1/4 cup	unsweetened (natural) smooth peanut butter	60 mL
2 tsp.	fresh ginger, crushed	10 mL
4	cloves garlic, crushed	4
1/4 cup + 2 Tbsp.	Indonesian Soy Sauce (p. 78)	90 mL
1/4 cup	water	60 mL

Whisk all ingredients together in a small bowl. Toss with steamed vegetables, fried tofu, or use as a dip.

Leftover sauce can be refrigerated in a sealed container for 5–7 days.

White Sauce

When you're not whipping up a batch of this to make Scalloped Potatoes (p.133) or Creamed Onions with Peas (p.137), use this mouthwatering sauce as a base in which to melt different kinds of cheeses, or as a decadent topping for just about any vegetable.

Makes 3 cups (750 mL)

3 Tbsp.	butter	45 mL
3 Tbsp.	flour	45 mL
3 cups	milk	750 mL
1/2 tsp.	salt	2.5 mL
pinch	pepper	pinch
2 Tbsp.	chopped parsley (optional)	30 mL

Melt the butter over medium heat in a medium saucepan. Remove from heat and whisk in the flour. Return to heat and whisk the milk in 1 cup (250 mL) at a time, making sure that no lumps remain as it heats. Heat to boiling, then reduce the heat and simmer, stirring constantly, until the sauce thickens, 4–6 minutes. Add salt and pepper, and parsley, if you like.

Cheese Sauce

This sauce carries off Macaroni and Cheese (p. 94) and Cauliflower au Gratin (p. 136). It's wonderful for just about any vegetable, from broccoli to Brussels sprouts, and it's so good that you may find yourself licking the plate.

Makes about 2 cups (500 mL)

¼ cup	butter	60 mL
¼ cup	flour	60 mL
1½ cups	milk	375 mL
dash	cayenne pepper	dash
pinch	dried parsley, or 1 Tbsp. (15 mL) finely chopped fresh parsley	pinch
1 cup	grated medium or old cheddar cheese	250 mL
	salt and pepper to taste	

Melt the butter in a medium saucepan over medium heat. Whisk in the flour, then gradually whisk in ³/₄ cup (185 mL) of milk.

Remove from heat and, still whisking, add cayenne, parsley, and cheese.

Return to the heat and add the rest of the milk, stirring until it starts to bubble. Let bubble for about 2 minutes, stirring constantly. Remove from heat and add salt and pepper to taste.

Creamy Sage-Whisky Sauce

This rich, velvety sauce, like the rosé sauce for Tomato-Cream Penne with Vodka on p. 95, uses evaporated milk with great success. If, however, you love using cream, feel free to substitute cream, partly or entirely. The combination of earthy sage and rosemary with the kick of whisky is extremely good. This sauce is wonderful over any type of pasta, and is very quick and easy to make.

Yields 3 cups (750 mL)

¹/₄ cup	butter	60 mL
¹/₄ cup	flour	60 mL
3 cups	2% evaporated milk	750 mL
1 cup	milk	250 mL
dash	freshly grated or ground nutmeg	dash
2 Tbsp.	whisky	30 mL
1 tsp.	dried sage	5 mL
1 tsp.	dried rosemary	5 mL
¹/₂ tsp.	salt	2.5 mL
pinch	pepper	pinch

Melt the butter in a medium saucepan over medium heat. Remove the pot from the heat, add flour, and whisk together to form a roux. Return to heat and let the roux bubble for 1–2 minutes. Gradually add the evaporated milk, whisking constantly. Add the regular milk and bring to a boil, whisking occasionally.

Reduce the heat to low and simmer, whisking occasionally, for 4–5 minutes, or until the sauce has thickened. Add the nutmeg and whisky, then sage and rosemary, rubbing dried herbs between your fingers as you add them. Let simmer for 2–3 minutes more.

Remove from heat and add salt and pepper. Serve immediately.

Golden Mushroom Gravy

As vegetarians, we don't serve gravy with our meals nearly often enough. This rich, golden gravy will make your mashed potatoes beam with pride. It's excellent with many of the main dishes in this book, too.

Makes about 2 cups (500 mL)

1 tsp. + 1 Tbsp.	olive oil	20 mL
2	small cloves garlic, crushed	2
1 cup	sliced mushrooms, packed	250 mL
2¹/₂ cups	vegetarian "chicken," vegetable, or onion stock*	625 mL
1¹/₂ Tbsp.	all-purpose flour	22.5 mL
pinch	each salt and pepper	pinch
1 tsp.	nutritional yeast flakes	5 mL

Heat 1 tsp. (5 mL) oil in a medium saucepan over medium heat. Add the garlic and mushrooms and sauté for 2–3 minutes. Add ¹/₄ cup (60 mL) stock and sauté for another 3–5 minutes, or until the mushrooms are soft.

Transfer the mushroom mixture to a food processor or blender. Add ¹/₂ cup (125 mL) stock and blend on high until it's completely smooth —about 1 minute.

Put the remaining tablespoon (15 mL) of oil in a saucepan and heat over medium-low heat. Add the flour and whisk together to form a roux. Add the mushroom mixture, salt, pepper, and yeast, stirring to combine thoroughly. Gradually add the rest of your stock, stirring constantly. If there are any lumps, whisk them out.

Heat the gravy to boiling. Boil for 1 minute, then reduce the heat to low and simmer for about 5 minutes, whisking occasionally, or until the gravy reaches the thickness you like. Add salt and pepper to taste. Extra gravy will keep refrigerated in an airtight container for 4–5 days.

*For a description of vegetarian "chicken" stock, please see page 22.

Barbecue Sauce

This sauce is so easy to make that you'll never have to buy the stuff in a bottle again. It's delicious brushed on veggie burgers or dogs, and enlivens a protein-rich side dish or sandwich filling when used as a marinade for tofu on p. 116.

Makes about ¾ cup (185 mL)

⅓ cup	ketchup	80 mL
1 Tbsp. + 2 tsp.	soy sauce	25 mL
1 Tbsp.	molasses	15 mL
1 tsp.	chili powder	5 mL
1	clove garlic, crushed	1
1 Tbsp.	water	15 mL
dash	cayenne	dash

Whisk together all ingredients in a medium bowl. This sauce keeps for a week in a covered container in the refrigerator, and also freezes well.

main courses

Skewer-Free Vegetable Satay

Traditionally, Indonesian satay consists of chunks of meat on a skewer, served with spicy peanut sauce. As vegetarians, we don't really need to run skewers through things, so I skipped that step in this recipe. This is wonderful over rice or rice noodles.

Serves 4-6

1 batch	Peanut Sauce (p. 79)	1 batch
4	cloves garlic, crushed	4
1/2 tsp.	cornstarch	2.5 mL
3/4 cup	vegetable stock (approx.)	185 mL
4 tsp.	peanut oil	20 mL
2	small onions, coarsely chopped	2
2	large carrots, peeled and julienned	2
4 cups	broccoli florets	1 L
2	red peppers, seeded and cut into 1 1/2-inch (4-cm) strips	2
3 cups	sliced mushrooms	750 mL
1/4 cup	soy sauce	60 mL
1	ripe avocado	1

In a small bowl, combine the peanut sauce, garlic, cornstarch, and 1/2 cup (125 mL) stock. Set aside.

Heat the oil in a wok or large, deep skillet over high heat. Stir-fry the onions and carrots for about 4 minutes, or until the onions have separated and started to brown.

Add the broccoli, peppers, and mushrooms and stir-fry for about 5 minutes, adding a little stock if the vegetables get too dry. Add the soy sauce and toss to coat.

Reduce the heat to medium-high and add the peanut sauce mixture. Toss to coat and simmer, stirring occasionally, for about 5 minutes, or until the vegetables are tender and the sauce has thickened.

Pit and peel the avocado, and cut it into thin slices. Serve satay over rice or rice noodles, and fan out avocado slices on the side of each plate.

Spicy Soy Stir-Fry

This delicious, satisfying stir-fry has it all—lots of nutritious vegetables, low-fat protein, and a spicy kick. Serve over rice or rice noodles.

Serves 4

1 cup	TVP chunks	250 mL
4	cloves garlic, minced	4
1 tsp.	crushed ginger	5 mL
1/4 cup	soy sauce	60 mL
2 Tbsp.	hoisin sauce	30 mL
1/2–3/4 tsp.	Korean chili paste	2.5–4 mL
1 1/2 cups	very hot vegetable stock	375 mL
1 1/2 tsp.	cornstarch	7.5 mL
1 Tbsp.	cold water	15 mL
1 Tbsp.	peanut oil	15 mL
2	medium carrots, peeled and sliced diagonally	2
2	large stalks celery, sliced	2
1	large head broccoli, cut into bite-size florets	1
2 cups	sliced mushrooms	500 mL
2 cups	bean sprouts, rinsed and dried	500 mL

Put the TVP chunks into a large bowl with the garlic, ginger, soy sauce, hoisin sauce, and chili paste. Add the hot stock and stir well to combine. Set aside, stirring occasionally, for at least 15 minutes as you chop the vegetables. Taste one TVP chunk to make sure that it's tender and hydrated. There should be liquid remaining in the bowl—this is your sauce. Put the cornstarch into a small bowl and add the cold water. Stir very well until the cornstarch is dissolved. Add the cornstarch solution to the TVP and stir to combine. Set aside.

Heat the peanut oil in a wok or large, deep skillet over medium-high heat. Add the carrots, celery, and broccoli, and stir-fry for 3–4 minutes. Add the mushrooms and stir-fry for another 3–4 minutes. If the vegetables get too dry, add 1–2 Tbsp. (15–30 mL) sauce from the TVP mixture.

Add the TVP chunks and sauce. Bring to a boil and let it fast-simmer for about 3 minutes, or until the sauce starts to thicken. Add the bean sprouts and stir-fry for another 2–3 minutes, or until the sauce has thickened and the bean sprouts have softened slightly.

Vegetable Pot Pie

Chicken pot pie was one of the meat dishes that lingered longest in my memory after I became vegetarian, and for a few years it seemed impossible to create a credible vegetarian version. But after a few tries, here it is—vegetables simmered in a creamy gravy topped with flaky pastry. This makes you feel better no matter what the ill— homesickness, a cold, a broken heart . . .

Serves 4–6

1 tsp.	butter	5 mL
3	small-to-medium onions, chopped	3
2	carrots, chopped	2
1	small-to-medium rutabaga, chopped into $1/2$-inch (1-cm) pieces (should yield 2 cups/500 mL)	1
2 cups	vegetable stock	500 mL
2	medium potatoes, chopped into $1/2$-inch (1-cm) pieces	2
1	bay leaf	1
$1/2$ tsp.	salt	2.5 mL
$1/4$ tsp.	thyme	1.2 mL
1 tsp.	Marmite	5 mL
1 Tbsp.	all-purpose flour	15 mL
$1/2$ cup	frozen peas	125 mL
$1/2$ cup	canned corn kernels, drained	125 mL
$1/2$ cup	milk	125 mL
$1/2$ batch	Basic/Savory Pastry (p. 27), chilled	$1/2$ batch

For the half batch of pastry, it's easier to make the whole batch, divide it in half, and put the other half in the freezer for another day.

Melt the butter in a large saucepan over medium heat. Add the onions, carrots, and rutabaga. Sauté, adding a little bit (2 Tbsp./ 30 mL) of stock at a time to keep the vegetables moist. Cook the onion mixture for 7–8 minutes, stirring frequently.

Add the potatoes, bay leaf, salt, thyme, and 1 cup (250 mL) of stock. Cover and reduce the heat to medium-low, uncovering and stirring occasionally, for about 15 minutes, or until the vegetables are cooked through.

Add the Marmite and stir to coat the vegetables. Then add the flour, stirring to coat. Stir in the peas, corn, and remaining stock. When the stock thickens and starts to bubble (about 3 minutes), add the milk. Reduce the heat to low and simmer for about 10 minutes, uncovered, to let the gravy thicken. If the vegetables are still a little undercooked, put the cover back on the pot and simmer for 4 or 5 minutes longer.

Roll out the pastry to fit a 2-quart (1.8-L) dish that is at least $2^{1}/_{2}$ inches (6.3 cm) deep. The pastry should be about 1 inch (2.5 cm) larger than the circumference of dish. (See the pastry tips on p. 29.)

Preheat the oven to 350°F (175°C). Remove the bay leaf from the vegetables and add salt and pepper to taste. Turn the mixture into your dish. Fold the pastry over your rolling pin and carefully lift it over the top of the dish. With a knife, trim the excess pastry from around the outside, but leave at least $^{1}/_{4}$ inch (.5 cm) extra—you will need this to seal the pastry onto the dish.

Press the pastry down against the edges of the dish to seal. If it's not sticking to the dish in places, moisten with a little bit of milk. If it's too small in spots, or if tears develop, see the milk-sealing trick in the pastry tips on p. 29. Once you're happy with it, brush the top with milk and cut a few slits in the pastry with a sharp knife to let steam escape.

Bake for about 30 minutes, or until the pastry is golden brown.

After talking with some baffled non-British friends, I think that some tips on rutabaga preparation are in order. Cut the ends off with a large knife. Peel with a potato peeler, making sure to peel off both the waxy outer skin and the greenish skin right underneath that.

Cheese and Green Onion Quiche

There is something very '80s about quiche, and for this reason quiches were not so popular for a while. Whether they're "in" now is something we shouldn't really waste our time with. All I can tell you is that your guests won't care once they try it. This simple version is extremely good—feel free to experiment with different kinds of cheese. Thanks to my mom for the idea.

Serves 4-6

¹/₂ batch	Savory Pastry (p. 27)	¹/₂ batch
1 tsp.	butter	5 mL
6	green onions, whites and half of greens, chopped	6
3	eggs	3
1¹/₄ cups	milk	300 mL
¹/₂ tsp.	salt	2.5 mL
pinch	pepper	pinch
1 cup	grated old cheddar	250 mL

Preheat the oven to 400°F (200°C). First, prebake your pie crust: Roll out the pastry to fit the pie plate, using the pastry tips from p. 29. Fold the pastry over the rolling pin, lift over the pie plate, and press it down into the plate. Using scissors, trim the outside to ¹/₄ inch (.5 cm) larger than the rim of the plate. Use your thumb to flute the edge, pressing down against the rim of the plate. Cut a piece of wax paper into a circle the size of the pie crust and lay it on the pastry. Fill the pastry with dried beans or pie weights, to prevent the crust from bubbling up while baking. If you are using beans, you can save them in a jar as your "pie weights" and reuse them forever. Bake for 10–12 minutes, or until the pastry is golden; lift up the beans and wax paper to check. Set aside to cool. Turn the oven down to 375°F (190°C).

Melt the butter in a medium skillet over medium heat. Add the green onions and sauté until they're softened and starting to brown, 4–5 minutes. Set aside.

Beat the eggs lightly in a medium bowl until uniform. Beat in the milk, salt, and pepper, then mix in the onions and cheddar.

Pour the egg mixture into the pie shell, using a fork or spoon to distribute the cheese and onions evenly.

Bake for 30–35 minutes, or until the top is golden and a knife inserted in the center comes out clean. Let cool for about 5 minutes before serving. Serve warm.

If you have never made a quiche before, take into account that it puffs up a good deal in the oven. Don't worry! You haven't done anything wrong. Quiches always do this. It will settle down again once you take it out of the oven.

Garden Pesto

This light, vegan pesto is loveliest in the summer, when basil and tomatoes are nicest and you're too hot to do a lot of cooking. Here's a sneaky trick that pinches pennies: use pecans or walnuts in the pesto rather than pine nuts. They add a wonderful richness and are much less expensive—and I always toast some pine nuts for garnish as a culinary foil.

Makes ¾ cup (185 mL) pesto, serving 4-6

2 cups	basil leaves, well rinsed, drained, and packed	500 mL
¼ cup	olive oil	60 mL
2 Tbsp.	nutritional yeast flakes	30 mL
¾ tsp.	salt	4 mL
1	clove garlic, coarsely chopped	1
¼ tsp.	pepper	1.2 mL
¼ cup	pecans, walnuts, or pine nuts	60 mL
¼ cup	pine nuts (optional)	60 mL
1 lb.	dried pasta	450 g
1	large tomato, chopped	1
1	avocado, peeled and chopped	1

Put the basil into a food processor with the olive oil, yeast, salt, garlic, pepper, and nuts. Process on high speed alternating with low (to get the ingredients incorporated) for about 1 minute. Then take the cover off the food processor and scrape down the sides with a rubber scraper. Process for another 30 seconds, or until the pesto looks uniform.

If you want to, roast the pine nuts on an ungreased baking sheet at 350°F (175°C) for no more than 4–5 minutes, and watch them closely. Once you can smell them roasting and they turn golden brown, they're ready. Take them out of the oven and spread them on a plate as soon as they're done, because they can turn from roasted to burnt in about a minute!

Cook the pasta in a large pot of boiling salted water until al dente, about 8 minutes. In a very large bowl, toss the pasta with the pesto, tomato, and avocado. If you have made the roasted pine nuts, sprinkle them on top. Serve immediately.

Avocados discolor very quickly after they've been cut, so always chop your avocados just before serving. If you're making more pesto than you need, don't chop extra avocados to go with it, as they will lend an unappetizing black color to your dish!

Macaroni and Cheese

For some unknown reason, people always think that making macaroni and cheese from scratch requires superhuman wit and dexterity. In fact, it's a pretty simple meal, and I guarantee you won't go back to the box after you try this recipe. It's rich, comforting, great for leftovers, and doesn't even need ketchup!

Serves 4-6

1 cup	macaroni, uncooked	250 mL
1 batch	Cheese Sauce (p. 80)	1 batch
1/2 cup	grated old or medium cheddar	125 mL

Preheat the oven to 400°F (200°C). Cook the macaroni in a large pot of boiling salted water until al dente, about 8 minutes. Drain.

Empty the macaroni into a 9- x 9-inch (23- x 23-cm) pan and pour cheese sauce evenly over the top. Sprinkle with the grated cheese. Place in the oven for 10 minutes to heat through, then place under the broiler for 5–10 minutes, or until golden brown on top.

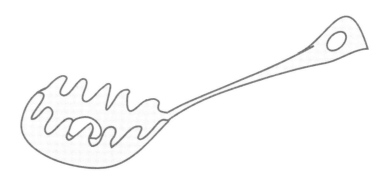

Tomato-Cream Penne with Vodka

This dish, officially known as Penne alla Vodka, is a staple on the menus of many posh Italian restaurants. The rosé sauce, however, is traditionally made with cream, which can taste extremely rich and make you feel a bit queasy afterwards. This version solves the richness dilemma by substituting evaporated milk for cream.

Serves 4–6

2	28-oz. (796-mL) cans peeled whole tomatoes, drained	2
2 cups	2% evaporated milk	500 mL
2 Tbsp.	olive oil	15 mL
8	cloves garlic, crushed	8
1 tsp.	salt	5 mL
1 tsp.	basil	5 mL
1/2 tsp.	oregano	2.5 mL
2 Tbsp.	vodka	30 mL
1 lb.	dried penne	450 g
	freshly ground black pepper	

Purée the tomatoes in a blender or food processor until smooth. Add the evaporated milk and blend until combined.

Put a large pot of salted water on to boil for the pasta.

Heat the olive oil over medium heat in a large, deep skillet or wok—either way, make sure it's large enough to hold the tomato mixture. Add the garlic and sauté for a minute or two—don't let the garlic brown. Add the tomato mixture and simmer, stirring occasionally. Don't be concerned if the sauce turns a bit foamy—this will disappear as it thickens. If the sauce starts to sputter, turn down the heat.

After about 15 minutes of simmering, add the salt, basil and oregano, crushing them between your fingers as you add them to bring out the flavors. Simmer for another 5 minutes.

Add the penne to the pot of boiling water and cook until al dente, about 8 minutes. Drain.

While the pasta is cooking, the sauce will have turned orange and should have reduced by about half. If it has not reduced this much, continue to simmer for another 5 minutes or so.

Stir in the vodka and simmer for another 5 minutes. Add freshly ground black pepper to taste. Ladle over the penne in shallow bowls.

Spaghetti with Tomato Sauce and Herbed Mushrooms

This dish goes well over just about any kind of pasta—though I always find spaghetti the most comforting. Don't let the simplicity of this meal fool you. It is extremely satisfying.

Serves 4–6

2 Tbsp.	olive oil	30 mL
8	cloves garlic, minced	8
2	28-oz. (796-mL) cans whole tomatoes	2
1/2 tsp.	maple syrup	2.5 mL
1/2 tsp.	oregano	2.5 mL
small pinch	chili flakes (optional)	small pinch
1 tsp.	basil	5 mL
1 1/4 tsp.	salt	6.2 mL
2 Tbsp.	red wine	30 mL
2 tsp.	butter	10 mL
4 cups	sliced mushrooms	1 L
1 lb.	dried spaghetti	450 g

Put a large pot of salted water on to boil for the pasta.

Heat the olive oil over medium heat in a large non-stick skillet that is at least 2 inches (5 cm) deep. Add the garlic and sauté for 1–2 minutes. With your hands, break up the tomatoes into the garlic and stir to combine. Set aside the juice from the cans.

Stir in the maple syrup, oregano, chili flakes if you're using them, half the basil, and 1 tsp. (5 mL) of the salt. Stir well and simmer, stirring occasionally, for about 15 minutes, then add the red wine.

Cook the spaghetti in boiling water until al dente, about 8 minutes. Drain.

While the pasta is cooking, simmer the sauce for another 5 minutes. If the sauce sputters, turn the heat down. The liquid should have decreased by about half. If the sauce has decreased too much, add a little tomato liquid.

While the sauce is simmering and the pasta is cooking, prepare the mushrooms. Melt the butter in a small non-stick skillet over medium heat. Add the mushrooms, remaining basil, and remaining $1/4$ tsp. (1.2 mL) salt and sauté for 5–7 minutes or until browned. If mushrooms brown too quickly and become dry, add a little bit of water.

Ladle the sauce over the spaghetti in shallow bowls. Spoon mushrooms over top.

Spaghetti "Bolognese"

The carnivorous version of this dish was about as Italian as my eating ever was when I was a kid. And it was my absolute favorite supper, whether I was being fed the slightly spicy and sweet version made by my dad, or the more aromatic, herb-filled version my mom whipped up. I think my version is somewhere between the two, and it remains one of the most comforting meals I make.

Serves 4

1 Tbsp.	olive oil	15 mL
1	medium onion, finely chopped	1
4	cloves garlic, crushed	4
$3/4$ tsp.	salt	4 mL
$1/2$ tsp.	oregano	2.5 mL
$1/2$ tsp.	thyme	2.5 mL
$1/2$ tsp.	chili powder	2.5 mL
1	28-oz. (796-mL) can diced tomatoes, with liquid, mashed slightly with potato masher	1
1 cup	TVP granules	250 mL
2 Tbsp.	ketchup	30 mL
$1/4$ cup	nutritional yeast flakes	60 mL
1 lb.	dried spaghetti	450 g

Put a large pot of salted water on to boil for the pasta.

Heat the oil in a deep skillet or wok over medium heat. Add the onion and garlic and sauté, stirring often, for about 5 minutes, or until softened. Add the salt, oregano, thyme, and chili powder, and sauté for another minute or so, until the onions are coated with spices.

Add the tomatoes and heat until bubbling. Add the TVP, ketchup, and yeast and simmer, stirring occasionally, for 15–20 minutes, or until the sauce has thickened.

While the sauce is thickening, cook the spaghetti for about 8 minutes in boiling water, or until al dente. Drain.

Ladle sauce over the spaghetti to serve.

Leftover sauce is a tacit invitation to make yourself a Sloppy Joe the next day. Heat sauce in a saucepan or the microwave. Cut a kaiser in half and lightly toast it. Top the kaiser with sauce, as well as a little grated cheddar, mozzarella, or gouda if you like. Eat with a knife and fork.

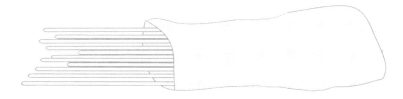

Fettuccine Primavera

This is a colorful, classy dish that's perfect for a dinner party. Feel free to make substitutions in vegetables, but I would leave in the artichokes and asparagus if I were you—they make the dish taste fancier.

Serves 4

3 Tbsp.	olive oil	45 mL
1	onion, coarsely chopped	1
4	cloves garlic, finely chopped	4
1	large carrot, julienned	1
1	head broccoli, cut into small florets	1
1 cup	sliced mushrooms	250 mL
20	asparagus spears, cut into thirds	20
1/2 tsp.	oregano	2.5 mL
1 tsp.	basil	5 mL
1/2 tsp.	salt	2.5 mL
1/2 cup	vegetable stock	125 mL
1 cup	canned artichoke hearts, drained and quartered	250 mL
3	medium-to-large tomatoes, diced	3
1/4 cup	red or white wine	60 mL
1 1/2 tsp.	nutritional yeast flakes	7.5 mL
1 lb.	dried fettuccine	450 g
	freshly ground black pepper	

Put a large pot of salted water on to boil for the pasta.

Heat the olive oil in a deep frying pan or saucepan over medium heat. Add the onions and garlic and cook, stirring frequently, for 2–3 minutes. Add the carrots, broccoli, mushrooms, asparagus, oregano, basil, and salt. Cook for 4–5 minutes, adding stock as you need it. Add the artichokes, tomatoes, wine, and yeast.

When the water is boiling, add the fettuccine and cook until al dente, about 8 minutes. Drain.

While the pasta is cooking, continue cooking the vegetables at medium heat, stirring frequently, for another 5 minutes, or until the vegetables are tender but not soft and the yeast has thickened the sauce.

Toss the vegetables in a large bowl with the fettuccine. Top with freshly ground black pepper to taste.

If you can't find fresh asparagus, try the frozen-food aisle—you'll be surprised at the quality of some frozen asparagus. But if you do buy frozen asparagus, keep in mind that it will take less time to cook, so let it defrost for a few minutes and add it at the same time as the artichokes.

Stuffed Peppers

Of all vegetarian standbys, stuffed peppers can definitely be the worst. I remember some terrible, bland things that someone brought to an Easter potluck in university. Though they were colorful and cheery-looking, they tasted so dismal that they drove me to sinful thoughts of glazed Easter ham. So here's my version. They're pretty, low in fat, and they taste as lively as they look.

Serves 4

1 1/2 cups	TVP granules	375 mL
2 Tbsp.	ketchup	30 mL
1 tsp.	chili powder	5 mL
1 tsp.	oregano	5 mL
1 1/2 cups	hot vegetable stock	375 mL
1 Tbsp.	olive oil	15 mL
1	large onion, diced	1
4	cloves garlic, crushed	4
2 1/2 cups	cooked rice, white or brown	625 mL
3/4 tsp.	salt	4 mL
1/2 cup	breadcrumbs	125 mL
1/4 cup	nutritional yeast flakes	60 mL
1/2 cup	corn kernels, canned or frozen	125 mL
	black pepper to taste	
4	large peppers, any color	4

In a large bowl, combine the TVP, ketchup, chili powder, and oregano. Add the vegetable stock, stir well, and let it sit.

Heat the olive oil over medium heat in a frying pan. Add the onion and garlic and sauté, stirring occasionally, for about 5 minutes or until soft.

Add the onions and garlic to the TVP mixture with the rice, salt, breadcrumbs, yeast, and corn kernels. Stir to combine and add black pepper to taste.

If your peppers topple over when you try to stand them up, cut a thin slice off the bottom until they're more self-sufficient. Don't cut too much, as you don't want any filling to fall through the bottom. Cut off the tops and run a thin knife around the central core of the peppers to remove the ribs and seeds. Shake out any remaining seeds.

Preheat the oven to 350°F (175°C). Stuff the peppers, packing in as much stuffing as you can. Put the peppers in a shallow baking dish with about $^3/_4$ inch (2 cm) of water in the bottom of the pan—this will keep the bottoms of the peppers from getting burned.

Cook the peppers for 1 hour, uncovered. Check after 40 minutes to see if the tops are getting too browned and dry; if they are, cover with aluminum foil for the last 20 minutes of baking.

Lasagne

What a crowd-pleaser of a dish! This version is always a hit, even for carnivores, because it offers the best of both worlds: the heartiness of a meat lasagne and the delicate flavor of a Florentine. I use light ricotta and mozzarella in this lasagne so as not to plug anyone's arteries too much—but it works just as well with the full-fat cheese if you can handle it!

Serves 6–8

2 Tbsp.	olive oil	30 mL
3	medium onions, diced	3
4	cloves garlic, minced	4
1/2 tsp.	salt	2.5 mL
2 tsp.	basil	10 mL
1 tsp.	oregano	5 mL
1 1/2 cups	vegetable stock	375 mL
2	28-oz. (796-mL) cans diced tomatoes	2
1/2 cup	tomato liquid from can	125 mL
1 Tbsp.	maple syrup	15 mL
1/4 cup	TVP granules	60 mL
4 cups	spinach leaves, rinsed, dried, chopped, and firmly packed	1 L
1	17-oz. (475-mL) container ricotta	1
3 cups	grated mozzarella	750 mL
12	oven-ready lasagne noodles	12

In a large saucepan over medium heat, heat the olive oil. Add the onions and garlic and sauté for 6–8 minutes, or until softened. Add the salt, 1 tsp. (5 mL) basil, 1/2 tsp. (2.5 mL) oregano, and 1/4 cup (60 mL) stock. Continue stirring for 2–3 minutes. Add the tomatoes and juice. Using a potato masher, mash the sauce until the tomatoes are in smaller pieces.

Reduce the heat to low and simmer for about 5 minutes. Add the maple syrup, TVP, and the rest of the stock. Simmer for about 10 minutes, stirring occasionally. The sauce will be watery-looking, which is fine—the oven-ready noodles need extra liquid. Add salt to taste.

In a very large bowl, combine the spinach with the ricotta, 1 tsp. (5 mL) of basil, $^1/_2$ tsp. (2.5 mL) oregano, and 2 cups (500 mL) grated mozzarella.

Preheat the oven to 350°F (175°C). Put enough sauce into a 13$^1/_2$- x 9.5-inch (34.5- x 24-cm) baking dish to cover the bottom. This should be no more than $^1/_3$ of the sauce. Cover this with a layer of noodles. The noodles should be about $^3/_4$ inch (2 cm) apart, since they will expand as they bake. Cover the noodles with half the spinach mixture, spreading evenly. Repeat the layers, finishing with a layer of noodles. Cover evenly with the rest of the sauce. Top with $^3/_4$ cup (185 mL) of mozzarella.

Cover and bake for 30 minutes. Remove from the oven, uncover, and use the remaining $^1/_4$ cup (60 mL) of cheese to patch up any spots on the top. Return to the oven for 15–20 minutes, or until the cheese is starting to brown. Let it sit for 5–10 minutes before serving.

This dish has a tendency to bubble over, so put a cookie sheet on a lower rack to protect your oven.

Eggplant "Parmesan"

The Casanova of meals. I came up with a dairy-free way of making this dish to serve a loved one who hates the strong taste of parmesan cheese, and it has served me well over the years, wowing many guests. While this recipe may be labor-intensive, it's worth the results, and far better than veal scallopine to seduce the one you love.

Serves 4-6

1	large eggplant, washed	1
2 Tbsp.	olive oil	30 mL
4	cloves garlic, minced	4
1	large onion, chopped	1
1 tsp.	salt	5 mL
2 tsp.	dried oregano	10 mL
1 tsp.	dried basil	5 mL
1	28-oz. (796-mL) can tomatoes, lightly mashed or chopped	1
1 Tbsp.	maple syrup	15 mL
3 Tbsp.	red wine	45 mL
1–1^1/$_2$ cups	flour	250–375 mL
^{1}/$_2$–^{3}/$_4$ cup	light vegetable oil	125–185 mL
^{1}/$_2$ cup	nutritional yeast flakes (approx.)	125 mL
4 Tbsp.	basil	60 mL

Cut off the ends of the eggplant and slice the eggplant into rounds no more than ^{1}/$_4$ inch (.5 cm) thick. To drain off bitter juices, place the eggplant slices in layers in a large colander, sprinkling each layer lightly with salt. Set the colander in a sink or large bowl to drain as you make the sauce.

In a medium saucepan, heat the olive oil over medium heat. Add the garlic and sauté no more than 30 seconds, or until you smell a rich garlic aroma. Add the onion and sauté for 2–3 minutes. Add 1 tsp. (5 mL) salt. Stir and add the oregano and 1 tsp. (5 mL) basil. Continue cooking for 3 minutes, stirring often, or until the onions and garlic are soft. Add the tomatoes and maple syrup. Bring the sauce to a gentle simmer, reducing the heat as needed. Add the red wine. Simmer gently for 10–15 minutes. Remove from the heat and set aside.

Spread 1 cup (250 mL) flour onto a large plate. In a frying pan, heat about 3 Tbsp. (45 mL) vegetable oil over medium-high heat. Start with 4–5 slices of eggplant, or whatever you think will fit in the frying pan side by side. Shaking each slice of eggplant to remove excess liquid, put the slices onto the flour and flip over, coating each side lightly. Shake off excess flour and place the slices in the pan. You might want to use two pans to speed up the process. Fry the eggplant until lightly browned on each side, adding oil as needed—never let the pan go dry, as it will begin to smoke. Don't be stingy with your oil!

While the first round of eggplant is frying, set up the next round in the flour. When the eggplant is brown on both sides, remove from the pan and set on a baking sheet covered with paper towel (this will absorb some of the oil). Put the next batch in the pan, adding more oil as needed, and continue until all are done. Add more flour to the plate if needed. Soon you will have elegant flour mittens on your hands, but this is half the fun. Add paper towel as needed between eggplant layers.

Preheat the oven to 350°F (175°C). In a 9- x 12-inch (23- x 30-cm) baking dish or approximate equivalent, spoon a thin layer of sauce in the bottom to keep the eggplant from sticking. Next, sprinkle about a tablespoonful (15 mL) of nutritional yeast over the sauce. Then, sprinkle a generous pinch of basil. Follow this with a layer of eggplant slices, overlapping the slices slightly so that there are as few gaps as possible. Follow with another layer of sauce, spreading the sauce evenly over the eggplant slices to cover them all. Add more yeast and basil. Repeat the layers until you run out of eggplant, finishing with a layer of sauce. Make sure that you reserve enough sauce to amply cover this top layer of eggplant. Finish by sprinkling with another generous pinch of yeast and basil.

Bake for 45 minutes, or until most of the liquid has been absorbed.

Sweet Potato Ravioli

I came up with this idea to help use up the piles of wrappers I always have left over when I make Egg Rolls (p.148). This recipe makes enough filling to feed 8–10 hungry people, but it's worth it to make more ravioli, as they freeze beautifully in resealable bags. Ravioli tastes good with a very simple tomato sauce, but is especially nice with the rosé sauce made for Tomato-Cream Penne with Vodka (p. 95), or Creamy Sage-Whisky Sauce (p. 81).

Makes 100–125 ravioli, serving 10 people

2	medium sweet potatoes, peeled and coarsely chopped	2
1 Tbsp.	butter	15 mL
1	clove garlic, sliced	1
1 cup	ricotta, regular or reduced-fat	250 mL
1/2 tsp.	salt	2.5 mL
1 Tbsp.	fresh chopped basil	15 mL
1/2 tsp.	dried oregano	2.5 mL
1/4 tsp.	pepper	1.2 mL
1	large package egg roll wrappers (at least 50)	1

Put the sweet potatoes in a saucepan and cover with water. Bring to a boil and boil gently until soft, about 15 minutes. Drain, and empty into a large bowl. Mash until quite smooth with a potato masher (a few lumps are all right). Set aside to cool.

Melt the butter in a small skillet or saucepan over medium-low heat. Add the garlic and sauté for 2–3 minutes, then drain the butter through a sieve to strain out the garlic. Let the butter cool slightly, then add to the sweet potatoes.

Add the ricotta, salt, basil, oregano, and pepper to the sweet potatoes and mix well. Taste, and add more salt if you like.

On your work surface, have a small bowl of water ready, and put 3–4 wrappers in a stack in front of you. Cut them into equal, square quarters by slicing the wrappers in half lengthwise, then in half cross-wise. Stack the quarters to one side, then lay pairs of them out in a row—do three or four pairs at a time.

Put about 1 tsp. (5 mL) filling into the center of one square, then dip your finger in water and run it all around the edges of the square. Run your finger the same way around the other square of the pair, then stick the two squares together, using your fingers to pinch and seal the edges. Use a knife to trim off any messy edges—just be sure not to trim off too much.

Repeat this process until you have as many ravioli as you like. Don't leave it out on the counter for more than 20 minutes, as the wrappers will start to dry out. The filling keeps for about 5 days in the refrigerator. Once the ravioli is made, it keeps very well in the freezer for up to 2 months. Ravioli can be cooked directly from frozen; it might take just a couple of minutes of extra boiling.

To cook, put the ravioli gently into salted boiling water and boil for 3-6 minutes—the cooking time will partly depend on the type of egg roll wrapper you're using. Remove one ravioli, cut into it, and taste to see if the wrapper is cooked. When cooked, drain and serve with your favorite pasta sauce. Each person should get 10–12 ravioli.

Cabbage Rolls

There used to be a little diner just off the highway between Orillia and Barrie, Ontario, that I remember stopping at when I was a kid during my annual trip to the Canadian National Exhibition in Toronto. The owners made wonderful cabbage rolls, succulently stewed in a spicy tomato sauce. I'm confident that this meatless version is faithful to the original.

Serves 6

1	large green cabbage, with outer leaves free of blemishes	1

Filling:

1 cup	TVP granules	250 mL
2 Tbsp.	ketchup	30 mL
1/2 tsp.	thyme	2.5 mL
1 tsp.	chili powder	5 mL
1/4 tsp.	black pepper	1.2 mL
3/4 tsp.	salt	4 mL
1 cup less 2 Tbsp.	hot vegetable stock	220 mL
2 tsp.	olive oil	10 mL
2	onions, chopped	2
3	cloves garlic, crushed	3
1	green pepper, seeded and chopped	1
2 1/2 cups	cooked white or brown rice	625 mL
1/4 cup	nutritional yeast flakes	60 mL

Sauce:

2 tsp.	olive oil	10 mL
3	cloves garlic, crushed	3
1	28-oz. (796-mL) can crushed tomatoes	1
3/4 cup	vegetable stock	185 mL
1/2 tsp.	salt	2.5 mL
1/2 tsp.	thyme	2.5 mL
1 1/2 tsp.	honey	7.5 mL
pinch	chili flakes	pinch

Rinse the cabbage well. Make a circular cut at the bottom of the cabbage, around the core—this will make it easier to remove the leaves. Put the cabbage, core down, into a large pot with about 2 inches (5 cm) of salted water in the bottom. Bring the water to a boil and then simmer, covered, for about 15 minutes, or until the outer leaves are tender. Drain the cabbage and fill the saucepan with cold water to cool the cabbage quickly.

Remove the cabbage from the water and carefully peel back the outer leaves one by one. Cut the thick central rib out of each leaf after you peel it off. Continue this until you have 8–10 large leaves—if the cabbage becomes too stiff, repeat the simmering process for another 5–7 minutes. Set the leaves aside.

Next, make the filling. In a large bowl, combine the TVP, ketchup, thyme, chili powder, pepper, and salt. Pour the stock over top and stir thoroughly. Set aside, stirring occasionally, for about 15 minutes.

Heat the oil in a large skillet over medium heat. Add the onions, garlic, and green pepper and sauté for 8–10 minutes or until the onions are browned, adding a little water if the vegetables get too dry. Add the onion mixture, rice, and yeast to the TVP, and stir to combine. Set aside.

To make the sauce, heat the oil in a medium saucepan over medium-low heat. Add the garlic and sauté for about 1 minute—don't let it brown. If the garlic starts to brown, take it off the heat immediately. Add the tomatoes, stock, salt, thyme, honey, and chili flakes, and simmer very gently for 6–8 minutes. Spread about $^1/_2$ cup (125 mL) sauce in the bottom of a 2-quart (1.8-L) baking dish with a lid.

Put between $^1/_3$ and $^1/_2$ cup (80–125 mL) filling into each cabbage leaf in a thick line, about $^1/_3$ of the way across the leaf. Fold the leaf over and roll up, tucking the ends in as you go. Repeat with each leaf, putting each finished roll seam side down into the casserole dish. When you have one layer of snugly fitted rolls, spread more sauce on top and start a new layer. When you have run out of cabbage leaves and filling, pour the remaining sauce over top.

Preheat the oven to 350°F (175°C). Bake, covered, for 30 minutes, then uncover and bake for another 30 minutes.

Shepherd's Pie

As a kid, I was always especially happy when we had shepherd's pie. Thanks to some experimenting, I still am. It's satisfying, delicious, and perfect for a cold winter's night. If you ever want to fool a carnivorous friend, this is the dish to do it with. My cats try to sneak bits of this, always a sign of a great recipe. It freezes well before and after it's been baked.

Serves 6–8

2 cups	TVP granules	500 mL
3 Tbsp.	ketchup	45 mL
1 Tbsp.	Marmite	15 mL
1/2 tsp.	salt	2.5 mL
2 cups	boiling water	500 mL
1 Tbsp.	olive oil	15 mL
3	medium onions, diced	3
1	large carrot, diced	1
1 1/4 cups	vegetable stock	300 mL
1/2 cup	frozen peas	125 mL
3/4 cup	canned corn, undrained	185 mL
1 1/2 Tbsp.	all-purpose flour	22.5 mL
1 batch	Mashed Potatoes (p. 132)	1 batch

Put the TVP, ketchup, Marmite, and salt in a medium bowl. Add the boiling water, stir well, and set aside, stirring occasionally.

Heat the olive oil in a large saucepan over medium heat. Add the onions and carrots. Cook until soft, 8–10 minutes. Add some stock as you need it to keep the mixture moist.

Stir in the TVP mixture. Add the peas, corn, and corn liquid. Cook over medium heat for about 5 minutes, stirring occasionally, until everything is hot and the liquid in the pot is bubbling. Add the flour, stirring well. Add the rest of the stock, stir well, and let simmer until the stock thickens, 6–8 minutes.

Preheat the oven to 350°F (175°C). Spoon the mixture into a 10- x 13-inch (25- x 33-cm) pan, or two smaller pans if you are planning to freeze one. Spread the mashed potatoes evenly over the TVP mixture, using a rubber spatula. For decoration, drag a fork across the potatoes to score the top.

Bake, uncovered, for 45–60 minutes, or until the top is slightly crispy and browned.

The Colonel's Tofu

Here's what you serve to someone who, whether having been a vegetarian for a month or a decade, still craves fried chicken. My belief is that nutritional yeast counts for at least three of those "secret herbs and spices" we were all told about. Eat this tofu with Mashed Potatoes (p. 132) and Golden Mushroom Gravy (p. 82), and be transported to Southern-fried heaven.

Serves 4

³/₄ cup	nutritional yeast flakes	185 mL
¹/₄ cup	breadcrumbs	60 mL
1 tsp.	dried parsley flakes, or 1 Tbsp. (15 mL) finely chopped fresh parsley	5 mL
³/₄ tsp.	salt	4 mL
¹/₂ tsp.	black pepper	2.5 mL
2	eggs	2
2 Tbsp.	milk	30 mL
¹/₄ cup	peanut or canola oil (approx.)	60 mL
16 oz.	extra-firm tofu, cut into 1¹/₂-x ¹/₃-inch (4- x 1-cm) slices	454 g

Prepare the breading by combining the yeast, breadcrumbs, parsley, salt, and pepper in a shallow bowl. Set aside. In a small bowl, lightly beat the eggs, and stir in the milk. Heat about 1 Tbsp. (15 mL) oil in a large, non-stick skillet over medium-high heat. If your skillet isn't non-stick, use more oil.

While the oil heats, start breading your tofu. Double-bread each slice: start by coating the tofu in breading—only a little bit will stick. Then transfer the slices to the egg wash and coat thoroughly. Return to the breading, and toss the breading over top to coat. Place as many slices in the skillet as will fit comfortably. Fry 3–4 minutes on each side, or until light brown and crispy. When cooked on both sides, transfer to paper towels to drain, then place on a cookie sheet in a 250°F (120°C) oven to keep warm. Continue with all the tofu slices, adding more oil as you need to. ***Don't be stingy with your oil***. The Colonel wasn't!

What better to sip leisurely while eating The Colonel's Tofu than a tall glass of homemade lemonade? Make it a real Southern affair! Here's how. In a pitcher, combine the juice of 3 lemons with 3 cups (750 mL) of water and $1/4$ cup + 2 Tbsp. (90 mL) white sugar. Serve over ice.

Barbecue Tofu

This tofu tastes great with corn on the cob and Colorful Coleslaw (p. 66) for a summertime dinner, and it also makes great leftovers for sandwiches, or shredded into wraps.

Serves 4–6

| 1 lb. | extra-firm tofu, rinsed and patted dry | 454 g |
| 1 batch | Barbecue Sauce (p. 83) | 1 batch |

Cut the tofu into slices $1/2$ inch (1 cm) thick and $1^1/2$ inches (4 cm) square. Combine the slices with barbecue sauce in a large bowl. Let the tofu marinate in the sauce for at least 20 minutes, tossing occasionally.

Preheat the oven to 375˚F (190˚C). Transfer the tofu slices to a non-stick baking sheet, or a baking sheet that's been well greased, leaving extra sauce in the bowl.

Bake, uncovered, for about 12–15 minutes, then remove from the oven and turn the slices over. Brush the other side liberally with the remaining sauce, and return to the oven for another 12–15 minutes.

Toad in the Hole

Thanks to the fantastic vegetarian products that have come on the market in the past couple of years, I can showcase one of my favorite British pub meals. I don't know why sausages are referred to as "toads," and it doesn't seem that anyone else does, either. Regardless, they're lovely when hidden in rich Yorkshire Pudding (p. 157) and served with vegetables and Golden Mushroom Gravy (p. 82).

Serves 4–6

1 Tbsp.	butter	15 mL
1 batch	Yorkshire Pudding batter (p. 157)	1 batch
12	vegetarian sausages	12

Preheat the oven to 375˚F (190˚C). Melt butter in a 6- x 10-inch (15- x 25-cm) dish in the oven. Remove the dish from the oven and pour the pudding batter in. Then drop the sausages one by one into the batter so that they form two rows of six.

Bake, uncovered, for about 30 minutes, or until the center is cooked and the edges have begun to brown. Serve in thick slices.

Indian-Spiced Lentil Stew (Dhal)

This is an easy recipe to prepare when you have canned goods on hand, but slim pickings in your crisper. It's delicious over rice or folded into a roti or tortilla, served with chutney and sliced bananas on the side.

Serves 4–6

1 Tbsp.	curry powder	15 mL
1/2 tsp.	ground cumin	2.5 mL
1/2 tsp.	turmeric	2.5 mL
1/2 tsp.	salt	2.5 mL
1	clove garlic, crushed	1
1 cup	soymilk	250 mL
1 Tbsp.	vegetable oil	15 mL
3	medium onions, chopped	3
1 1/2	28-oz. (796-mL) cans diced tomatoes	1 1/2
1/4 cup	tomato liquid from can	60 mL
1	19-oz. (540-mL) can lentils, drained	1

In a small bowl, combine the curry powder, cumin, turmeric and salt. Add the garlic. Gradually add the soymilk, stirring with a fork to combine well. Set aside.

Heat the oil in a large saucepan over medium-low heat. Add the onions and sauté, stirring occasionally, for about 12 minutes, or until they're soft and just starting to brown.

Add the soymilk mixture to the onions. Cook until the soymilk starts to thicken and bubble, about 3 minutes. Add the tomatoes and juice, using a potato masher to mash the tomatoes into smaller pieces. Add the lentils, stir, and simmer uncovered for about 15 minutes.

D.I.Y. Pizza

If you have a little tomato sauce and some leftover vegetables and cheese handy, you've got pizza. The trick to making expert, delicious pizza at home is to always have packets of yeast in the cupboard. Yeast packets usually come in sets of three, and are called "active dry yeast." I like to put rosemary in my pizza crust, but feel free to use oregano, basil, or thyme instead.

Serves 4-6

Pizza Crust:

1¹/₄ cups	lukewarm water	300 mL
2 tsp.	active dry yeast (1 packet)	10 mL
pinch	sugar	pinch
1 tsp.	salt	5 mL
1¹/₂ tsp.	chopped fresh rosemary, or 1 tsp. (5 mL) dried	7.5 mL
3 cups	all-purpose flour	750 mL
3 Tbsp.	olive oil	45 mL

Toppings:

³/₄–1 cup	tomato sauce	185–250 mL
2 cups	grated mozzarella, cheddar, or havarti (approx.)	500 mL
	thinly sliced tomato, sliced artichoke hearts, sliced mushrooms, olives, thinly sliced onions, chopped green or red peppers	

Put the water in a small bowl, then add the yeast and sugar. Stir well until the yeast is dissolved. Let it sit for 5–7 minutes, or until the liquid has turned bubbly.

In a large bowl, combine the salt, rosemary, and 1 cup (250 mL) flour. Pour in the yeast mixture, as well as 1 Tbsp. (15 mL) oil. Stir until combined. Gradually add the rest of the flour, using your hands to mix the flour in toward the end. To incorporate the last bits of flour, really work the dough into the flour.

Lightly flour your counter or work surface, and knead the dough for about 5 minutes, using the heel of your hand to press the dough down and away from you, then rotate the dough and repeat. Don't be afraid to use pressure.

Put 1 Tbsp. (15 mL) oil into a large bowl, and spread it around the bottom and sides. Put the dough in the bowl, turning it over and rotating it so that all of the dough is greased. Cover with plastic wrap and put in a warm place with no drafts for about $1\frac{1}{2}$ hours, or until doubled in size.

Punch down the dough with your fist, then return it to your lightly floured surface. If you want to freeze the dough, now's the time to do it—wrap it very well in plastic wrap or put into a resealable bag and squeeze all the air out of the bag before you close it. To thaw the pizza dough, coat the frozen dough in olive oil, then place in a large bowl at room temperature or slightly warmer, covered tightly with plastic wrap. It will take about 5 hours to thaw. Alternatively, you can remove the dough from the freezer the day before and let it thaw by placing in the refrigerator. Then let it reach room temperature the next day in a covered bowl.

Keep the dough in one ball for one large rectangular pizza the size of a $12\frac{1}{2}$- x 17-inch (32.5- x 43-cm) baking sheet, or separate into smaller balls for smaller pizzas. You can stretch this dough to fit whatever shape you like, so you can use whatever baking sheets you have on hand.

(Continued on next page)

Knead the dough for about 3 minutes, then cover it loosely with plastic wrap and let it sit for 10–15 minutes more. Rub the dough with the remaining olive oil, and use the heel of your hands to stretch it into the shape of your baking sheet, pushing outward from the center. This will take some patience, but it will become easier to stretch after 2–3 minutes of work. Stretch until your dough is no more than $1/2$ inch (1 cm) thick, with thicker edges to hold in the tomato sauce.

Preheat the oven to 475°F (245°C). Spread the tomato sauce over the dough, going right out to the edges. Sprinkle with grated cheese, then top with whatever toppings you like.

Bake in the center of the oven for 15–20 minutes, or until the cheese is bubbling and starting to brown and the edge of the crust is golden brown. Remove from the oven and cut in half to test that the dough is cooked in the center. If it still looks doughy and uncooked, return to the oven for a few minutes.

Let sit 5 minutes before serving.

There are two tomato sauces in this book that make excellent pizza sauce: the sauce for Eggplant "Parmesan" on p. 106, and the sauce for Cabbage Rolls on p. 110. The next time you're making a tomato sauce, make double, and freeze the extra sauce in small quantities. This way, you can defrost just as much sauce as you need for your pizza.

Veggie Burgers

Why is it so important for vegetarians to be able to eat burgers? I think there's a one-word answer to this question: integration. I can't count the number of times I've eaten veggie burgers in pubs with beer-swilling, meat-eating friends. All the ingredients—less the water—can be combined and stored in an airtight container for weeks, making them a great instant food for camping trips or cottaging.

Serves 6

1 cup	TVP granules	250 mL
1/4 cup	rolled oats	60 mL
1/4 cup	walnuts	60 mL
1/3 cup	gluten flour	80 mL
1/2 cup	whole wheat flour	125 mL
1 tsp.	salt	5 mL
1 tsp.	chili powder	5 mL
1/2 tsp.	thyme	2.5 mL
1/2 tsp.	paprika	2.5 mL
1/4 cup	nutritional yeast flakes	60 mL
1 Tbsp.	vegetarian stock mix	15 mL
pinch	pepper	pinch
1 1/4 cups	boiling water	300 mL
	olive or vegetable oil for frying	

Preheat the oven to 375°F (190°C). Put the TVP into a food processor and process on low speed until the granules are a smaller size, but are not completely powdery, about 10 seconds. Put into a large bowl. Repeat this step with the rolled oats and the walnuts, processing each separately until they are in small bits but aren't a fine powder. Add to the bowl.

Mix in all remaining ingredients except oil, adding the boiling water last.

Heat the olive or vegetable oil in a skillet over medium-high heat. As there is no oil in the mix, some oil in the pan is necessary. Form the mix into patty shapes with your hands. Fry evenly on both sides until browned, 5–7 minutes total.

Alternately, grease a baking sheet and bake the burgers, uncovered, for 20–25 minutes, turning once halfway through.

Extra burger mix, once the water is added, can be wrapped in plastic wrap in a patty shape and refrigerated for up to 5 days.

Hearty Chili

This recipe is the result of years of chili-making on my part, and I hope it lives on as a force of change in the world of meatless chili. It's extremely high in fibre without tasting virtuous—the peanut butter gives it a lovely rich taste. Leftovers freeze well as long as the sweet potatoes are chopped into small pieces; otherwise they go a bit spongy. If you can't find bulgur or if you're dead set against it, just use another $1/4$ cup (60 mL) of TVP.

Serves 6

1 Tbsp.	olive oil	15 mL
2	medium onions, chopped	2
2	stalks celery, finely chopped	2
1	large sweet potato, peeled and chopped into $1/2$-inch (1-cm) cubes (about 2 cups/500 mL)	1
2	28-oz. (796-mL) cans diced tomatoes	2
4	cloves garlic, crushed	4
2	19-oz. (540-mL) cans red kidney beans, black beans, chickpeas, or bean medley, drained and rinsed	2
2 Tbsp.	chili powder	30 mL
1 tsp.	salt	5 mL
$1/2$ cup	canned corn kernels, with $1/4$ cup (60 mL) liquid from can	125 mL
$1/2$ cup	TVP granules	125 mL
$1/4$ cup	medium or coarse bulgur wheat	60 mL
$1/4$ cup	peanut butter, smooth or crunchy	60 mL

Heat the oil in a large saucepan. Add the onions and celery and sauté, stirring occasionally, for about 5 minutes. Add the sweet potato and continue to sauté, adding a little water if the mixture gets too dry.

After 5–7 minutes of sautéeing, add the tomatoes with their liquid. Reduce the heat to medium-low and stir in all of the remaining ingredients. Stir very thoroughly after you add the peanut butter, making sure that it dissolves and there aren't any lumps of it left.

Simmer partially covered, stirring occasionally, for about 40 minutes or until the sweet potatoes are soft.

If you have lots of chili left over, try baking it into a delicious savory pie. Prepare one batch of Basic/Savory Pastry Dough (p. 27). Roll out the base as directed in the recipe, and fill right to the top with chili. Roll out the top and place over the filling as directed in pastry recipe. Bake at 375°F (190°C) for 35–40 minutes, or until the center of the pastry top is golden.

Complete Taco Dinner

Tacos are a great Friday night dinner: they're easy to make, impressive, and can be easily customized for different guests and tastes. This taco "meat" is delicious and really rounds out the experience!

Serves 4-6

"Meat":

1½ cups	TVP granules	375 mL
2½ tsp.	chili powder	12.5 mL
¼ tsp.	salt	1.2 mL
½ tsp.	dried thyme	2.5 mL
1½ cups	boiling hot vegetable stock	375 mL
1 Tbsp. + 2 tsp.	ketchup	25 mL
2 tsp.	olive oil	10 mL
1	medium onion, finely chopped	1
2	cloves garlic, crushed	2
2 Tbsp.	soy sauce	30 mL
1–2	4.6-oz. (125-g) boxes taco shells (12 per box, 3–4 per person)	1–2

Toppings:

1 batch	Guacamole (p. 77)	1 batch
2	tomatoes, diced	2
1	onion, very finely chopped	1
2–3 cups	lettuce, shredded	500–750 mL
2 cups	grated cheddar cheese	500 mL
1 cup	salsa	250 mL

In a medium bowl, combine the TVP, chili powder, salt, and thyme. If you're using powdered stock, add the amount of stock powder needed for $1^1/_2$ cups (375 mL) at this stage—this will save you from mixing up stock in a separate bowl. Add the boiling stock or water, and stir to combine. Add the ketchup. Set aside for 10–15 minutes, stirring occasionally.

Heat the olive oil over medium-high heat in a large skillet. Add the onion and garlic and sauté until browned, 7–9 minutes, adding a little water if the mixture gets too dry.

Reduce the heat to medium, add the soy sauce, and stir to coat the onions and garlic. Add the TVP and sauté for 3–4 minutes, or until heated through.

Put the toppings in separate bowls for guests to pick and choose. Heat the taco shells at 375°F (190°C) for 3–5 minutes, or as directed on the box.

vegetables

Asparagus in Lemon-Garlic Butter

There's nothing nicer than asparagus when it's in season. Toss aside your knife and fork and eat with your fingers.

Serves 4

2 bunches	asparagus, washed (about 40 spears)	2 bunches
2 Tbsp.	butter	30 mL
4	cloves garlic, thinly sliced	4
2 tsp.	lemon juice	10 mL
	salt and pepper	

To remove the tough ends from asparagus, hold a couple of spears in your hands at a time and snap the ends off like you would a twig.

Steam the asparagus until tender but not entirely soft, 6–8 minutes.

While the asparagus is steaming, make the sauce. In a small sauce-pan or skillet, melt the butter over medium heat. Add the garlic and sauté for about 3 minutes, or until the garlic has softened slightly—don't let it brown. Remove from the heat and add the lemon juice. Stir for about 30 seconds. Return to the heat for a minute or so, until the sauce starts to bubble.

Arrange the asparagus on a platter, or on separate plates for individual servings. Drizzle the sauce on top. Sprinkle with salt and pepper.

Glazed Carrots

Even people who say they hate cooked carrots will eat them this way. Buttery, sweet, and simple, this dish is a classic.

Serves 4–6

6	medium carrots, peeled and sliced into $^1/_2$-inch (1.2-cm) rounds (about 3 cups/750 mL)	6
2 Tbsp. + $^1/_4$ cup	packed brown sugar	90 mL
2 Tbsp.	butter	30 mL
$^1/_4$ tsp.	salt	1.2 mL
large pinch	black pepper	large pinch

Put the carrots in a saucepan and cover them with water. Add 2 Tbsp. (30 mL) packed brown sugar, and stir to combine. Bring the carrots to a boil and simmer until tender, 6–10 minutes. Drain, reserving about 2 Tbsp. (30 mL) of the carrot liquid.

In a saucepan, melt the butter over medium heat. Stir in the remaining $^1/_4$ cup (60 mL) of brown sugar with the carrot liquid. Let bubble for 3–4 minutes, or until thickened slightly. Add the carrots, salt and pepper, and toss to coat. Sauté for 1–2 minutes, or until the carrots are thoroughly heated through. Serve hot.

Spinach in Broth

I have always liked cooked spinach, and this is a simple but tasty way to prepare it. However, I would shy away from serving it to people when you're not sure of their leanings towards this nutrient-rich green. Some people just hate cooked spinach, and will never change their minds. You can't change the world, but you can feel Popeye-like and strong from eating this dish.

Serves 4–6

1 cup	vegetable stock	250 mL
6 cups	spinach leaves, washed, dried, and packed	1.5L
pinch	each salt and pepper	pinch

Heat $^1/_2$ cup (125 mL) stock over medium-high heat in a deep skillet or wok. Add the spinach gradually in large handfuls; it's a lot of bulk to begin with but will reduce dramatically.

Once it's reduced a bit (3–4 minutes), add the rest of the stock and stir. Reduce the heat to medium and simmer for 5–7 minutes, or until the stock has reduced. Add salt and pepper to taste.

Mashed Swede

"Swede" is known as "rutabaga" in North America. This is a fantastically comforting vegetable, ranking right up there with Mashed Potatoes (p. 132). My family serves this as a side dish at all important meals, from Christmas to Easter to Thanksgiving. However, I have been known to eat large bowls of swede as a meal in itself.

Serves 4-6

1	large swede, peeled and chopped into 1-inch (2.5-cm) pieces	1
2 tsp.	butter	10 mL
1/2 cup	onion soup, made from onion soup mix	125 mL
3/4 tsp.	salt	4 mL
1/2 tsp.	pepper	2.5 mL

Boil the swede gently in a large saucepan with plenty of water until it has turned a rich orange color and is completely soft, about 30 minutes. Drain and return to the saucepan.

Add the butter and mash, using a potato masher. Get the mixture as smooth as possible, although a few lumps are all right if you're feeling lazy. Stir in the soup, salt, and pepper.

If you don't have onion soup mix available, you can prepare swede the traditional way, which is delicious but higher in fat: use butter instead. For one large swede, you would need at least 3 Tbsp. (45 mL) butter. Add more to taste if you dare!

Baked Acorn Squash

My dad makes this often in his restaurant, to go with roast beef or some other Sunday-type dinner. I absolutely love squash this way; it's caramel-tasting but not too sweet, and it's deliciously buttery. This is an excellent vegetable to serve at Christmas or Thanksgiving dinner.

Serves 4-6

1	medium acorn squash, about 4–5 inches (10–12 cm) in diameter	1
4 tsp.	butter	20 mL
1 Tbsp.	brown sugar	15 mL
large pinch	each salt and pepper	large pinch

Preheat the oven to 350°F (175°C). Cut the squash in half lengthwise. Using a soup spoon, scoop out the seeds from the center of each half. Place the halves, cut side down, on a baking dish that's just big enough to fit them, with about 1 inch (2.5 cm) of water in the bottom. Cook the squash, uncovered, for 25 minutes.

Remove from the oven and use an oven mitt and a spatula to remove the squash halves and flip them over. Empty the water from the dish. Return the squash to the dish, cut side up, and place half the butter and sugar in each hollowed-out center. Put a generous pinch of salt and pepper in each half.

Some of the butter will melt right away due to the heat of the squash; use this to brush all over the cut parts of the squash. Return to the oven and cook for 40 minutes, removing from the oven and brushing every 10 minutes or so.

Increase the heat to 375°F (190°C) and bake for another 20–30 minutes, basting every 10 minutes, until the squash has turned dark orange and started to caramelize. Insert a skewer or chopstick into the squash to make sure that it's soft all the way through. Cut each half into 2 or 3 slices right in the dish to catch the glaze. Arrange the slices on a plate and drizzle the glaze over. Serve.

Mashed Potatoes

This version, which can be made with vegan margarine instead of butter, has all of the richness of traditional mashed potatoes without the milk. Delicious with Golden Mushroom Gravy (p. 82).

Serves 4–6

6	medium-to-large potatoes, peeled and cut into uniform pieces	6
2 tsp.	butter	10 mL
1/2–3/4 cup	vegetable stock	125–185 mL
pinch	each salt and pepper	pinch

Place the potatoes in a large saucepan and cover with water. Bring to a boil, and cook until the potatoes are soft, about 15 minutes. Drain and mash them with butter in the pot. With a wooden spoon, mix in enough stock to make them look whipped and smooth rather than lumpy. Add salt and pepper to taste.

New Potatoes with Parsley

This dish is simple, but you can't go wrong with it: lovely little new potatoes in a rich, buttery parsley glaze.

Serves 4–6

20	new potatoes, scrubbed, with eyes and blemishes removed	20
1/4 cup + 2 Tbsp.	butter	90 mL
1 cup	chopped fresh parsley	250 mL

Cover the potatoes with water in a large saucepan. Bring to a boil, and boil gently for 20–25 minutes, or until the potatoes are completely cooked through. To test, remove the largest potato and cut it in half. Drain the potatoes.

Return your saucepan to the stove and melt the butter over medium-low heat. Add the parsley and sauté for about a minute, or until soft. Add the potatoes and toss to coat.

Scalloped Potatoes

This definitely ranks among the most comforting dishes ever made. If you didn't grow up eating scalloped potatoes, by all means reinvent your childhood by making these now and repeating as often as possible. There is an alchemy of sorts with this recipe. It goes in the oven as humble layers of potatoes and onions topped with white sauce. It comes out as bliss.

Serves 6–8

6	medium potatoes, peeled and sliced as thinly as possible	6
1	medium onion, peeled and sliced as thinly as possible	1
	salt and pepper for sprinkling	
1 Tbsp.	butter	15 mL
1 batch	White Sauce (p. 79)	1 batch

Preheat the oven to 350°F (175°C). Butter a 9- x 11-inch (23- x 28-cm) baking dish. Spread with alternating layers of potato and onion slices, sprinkling each potato layer with salt and pepper. Finish with a potato layer. Dot the top with 1 Tbsp. (15 mL) butter. Slowly and evenly pour the white sauce over top.

Cover and bake for 45 minutes. Take the cover off and bake for another 45–60 minutes, or until the top has started to turn brown in spots.

Two-Tone Oven Fries

These are a favorite with everyone who tries them. They'll make you feel better about yourself than caving in at that chip stand, too.

Serves 4

2 Tbsp.	vegetable oil	30 mL
1/2 tsp.	chili powder	2.5 mL
1/2 tsp.	salt	2.5 mL
1	large clove garlic, crushed	1
1	large sweet potato, peeled and cut into 1/4- x 3-inch (.5- x 7.5-cm) pieces	1
3	medium potatoes, scrubbed and cut into same size as sweet potato	3

Preheat the oven to 400°F (200°C). Combine the oil, chili powder, salt, and garlic in a large bowl. Gradually stir the potatoes into this mixture as you chop them—this will make them easier to coat.

Spread them out on one large cookie sheet or two smaller ones. Some fries can be resting on top of each other, but it shouldn't be too crowded on there.

Bake for about 30 minutes. After about 15 minutes, they should be cooked but not soft—take them out and, using a sturdy pancake flipper, loosen them and flip them over. After about 30 minutes, they should be browned and slightly crispy.

Serve with ketchup and mayonnaise for dipping, or drizzle Golden Mushroom Gravy (p. 82) over top.

These fries are low in oil, which means they like to stick to the pan if you're not using one with 3 layers of non-stick coating. It's all right if they stick—this actually gives them a nice crispiness. But be prepared: I use an old cookie sheet without a non-stick coating just for these fries—I make them often enough to warrant it! Also, use a metal or melamine pancake flipper to turn the fries over, rather than a softer plastic one. This will help you pry them off the cookie sheet more easily.

Bubble and Squeak

This dish combines humble ingredients to create something fabulously comforting. It's also a great way of using up leftover mashed potato and veg (you can substitute Brussels sprouts for the cabbage). The Brits are divided on the origin of the name of this food, but most concur that it bubbles in the pan, and squeaks in your mouth (the cabbage, that is). Make sure you have your ketchup handy.

Serves 4–6

3 cups	finely chopped uncooked cabbage, or 2 cups (500 mL) finely chopped cooked cabbage	750 mL
5–7 tsp.	butter	25–35 mL
1	large onion, finely chopped	1
2 cups	Mashed Potatoes (p. 132)	500 mL
2	eggs, lightly beaten	2
1/2 tsp.	salt	2.5 mL
1/4 tsp.	pepper	1.2 mL

If your cabbage is uncooked, bring a medium pot of water to the boil and put the cabbage in. Boil gently for 5–7 minutes, or until tender. Drain and set aside.

Melt 1 tsp. (5 mL) butter in a skillet over medium heat. Add the onions and sauté for 6–8 minutes, or until browned, adding a little water if the onions become too dry.

In a large bowl, combine the cabbage, onion, potato, eggs, salt, and pepper.

Melt about 2 tsp. (10 mL) butter in your skillet over medium-high heat. Drop the mixture by 1/4 cupfuls (60 mL) into the skillet, and flatten slightly into patties. Fry for about 5 minutes on each side, or until well browned and crispy. For each round of patties, add more butter to your skillet. Serve hot with ketchup or Golden Mushroom Gravy (p. 82).

Like about half the people who make bubble and squeak, I've put eggs into the mixture to hold it together. If you are vegan, you can cook this the way the other half does: forego the eggs and sauté it in the skillet until it's browned.

Cauliflower Au Gratin

This was a dish that I would often ask my mom to make when I was growing up—and now my niece, Rebecca, badgers the poor woman with the same demand. Although this is technically a side dish, I often eat it as a main course with a tossed salad and bread.

Serves 4-6

1	medium head cauliflower, cut into 2-inch (5-cm) florets	1
1 batch	Cheese Sauce (p. 80)	1 batch
³/₄ cup	grated old or medium cheddar	185 mL
1 Tbsp.	finely chopped fresh parsley (optional)	15 mL

Preheat the oven to 375°F (190°C). Gently boil the cauliflower in a large pot of salted water for 6–8 minutes, or until tender but not soft. Drain.

Turn the cauliflower into a buttered 7- x 9-inch (18- x 23-cm) dish. Pour the cheese sauce over top, and toss gently to coat the cauliflower.

Bake, uncovered, for about 20 minutes, or until the sauce is bubbling and the cauliflower is starting to brown. Remove from the oven and sprinkle the cheddar and parsley, if using, evenly over top.

Return to the oven and bake another 10 minutes, or until the cheese has started to brown. Remove from the oven and let sit about 5 minutes before serving.

Creamed Onions with Peas

Don't turn away from this dish because of its humble title. It tastes fantastic, and is a wonderful side dish for a special occasion.

Serves 6

6	medium onions, peeled and ends cut off	6
1¹/₂ cups	frozen peas	375 mL
¹/₄ tsp.	salt	1.2 mL
¹/₄ tsp.	pepper	1.2 mL
1 batch	White Sauce (p. 79), made with 3 Tbsp.(45 mL) chopped fresh parsley	1 batch

Cut onions into quarters. Bring a large pot of salted water to a boil. Add the onions and boil gently, uncovered, until they are very tender and have started to separate, about 15 minutes. Drain the onions and set aside, but first see the sidebar.

Preheat the oven to 350°F (175°C). Empty the onions and peas into a buttered 2-quart (1.8-L) dish. Sprinkle with salt and pepper. Pour the white sauce evenly over the vegetables, using a spatula or spoon to spread it out to cover all the vegetables.

Bake, uncovered, for about 30 minutes. Let sit for 5 minutes before serving.

You may want to save the water in which you boil the onions. It's extremely flavorful and makes wonderful stock if you simmer it with some of the vegetables mentioned on p. 26.

side dishes

Roasted Garlic

Whenever you're having cheese and crackers, fresh crusty bread, or a pasta that will need a little extra something, throw some heads of garlic into the oven. When roasted, garlic becomes mellow, sweet, and rich, and spreads beautifully. This is a great way to make a dinner special without spending a lot of money or time.

Serves 4-6

4	heads garlic, unblemished and firm	4
3 tsp.	olive oil (approx.)	15 mL
	salt and pepper	

Preheat the oven to 400°F (200°C). Cut the very tops off the heads of garlic, so that you've exposed most of the cloves. Remove excess paper from the heads, but make sure the heads are still well contained in their paper skins.

Cut a large piece of aluminum foil. Fold it in half so it's double-thick. Arrange the garlic, tops up, in the center of the foil.

Drizzle about $3/4$ tsp. (4 mL) of olive oil over each head of garlic, trying to coat the top of each exposed clove. Sprinkle each head liberally with salt and pepper.

Gather the foil at the top and center of the heads of garlic and scrunch up to close—the bundle should look like a big chocolate kiss.

Roast for about 40 minutes, or until the garlic is completely soft and the tops have started to go brown. Let cool slightly. Remove from the foil and serve as is. To eat, simply remove the cloves and squeeze out of the paper skins.

Faux Gras (Veggie Pâté)

I've been working on this recipe for years, and the ultimate test of this final version occurred at a New Year's party, when a non-vegetarian guest said in disbelief, "This is *vegetarian*?" This pâté is wonderful in sandwiches and on crackers, and also makes an elegant, light meal when it's sliced thinly over salad. It freezes perfectly wrapped in aluminum foil.

Makes one 8- x 10-inch (20- x 25-cm) pan

2	medium sweet potatoes, peeled and coarsely chopped (about 3 cups/750 mL)	2
1 cup	unsalted sunflower seeds	250 mL
1/2 cup	chopped walnuts	125 mL
1	medium onion, chopped	1
3	cloves garlic, coarsely chopped	3
10	mushrooms, coarsely chopped	10
1 cup	vegetable or onion soup stock	250 mL
1/2 cup	whole wheat flour	125 mL
2/3 cup	nutritional yeast flakes	160 mL
1 Tbsp.	olive oil	15 mL
1 tsp.	each oregano and thyme	5 mL
1 tsp.	salt	5 mL
1/2 tsp.	pepper	2.5 mL

Boil the sweet potatoes gently for 10–15 minutes, or until soft. Drain and set aside. In a food processor, grind the sunflower seeds and walnuts until they form a fine meal. Put into a large bowl.

Put the sweet potatoes, onion, garlic, and mushrooms into the food processor. Add about 1/2 cup (125 mL) of the stock and process on high speed until the vegetables form a smooth purée, about 3–4 minutes. If they're not blending smoothly, add a little more stock.

Add the purée to the nut meal in the large bowl. Mix in the flour, yeast, oil, oregano, thyme, salt, pepper, and remaining stock. Preheat the oven to 350°F (175°C). Turn the mixture into an oiled 8- x 10-inch (20- x 25-cm) dish, and spread evenly with a spatula. Sprinkle with a little nutritional yeast and thyme for garnish, if you like.

Bake for 60–75 minutes, or until the center feels crispy. Let cool thoroughly, preferably overnight. The pâté will firm up as it cools.

Stuffed Mushrooms

This is the perfect finger food for parties. The following is a pretty straightlaced version, but it's a classic and is absolutely delicious. For a change, feel free to tart up the filling a bit with some grated gruyère or gouda.

Serves 4–6

16	white, unblemished button mushrooms with caps, $1^1/_2$ inches (4 cm) in diameter (approx.)	16
4 Tbsp.	butter	60 mL
$^1/_4$ cup	finely chopped onion	60 mL
1	large stalk celery, finely chopped	1
$^3/_4$ cup	fresh, soft breadcrumbs	185 mL
1 Tbsp.	finely chopped fresh parsley	15 mL
$^1/_4$ tsp.	salt	1.2 mL
large pinch	pepper	large pinch

Wash the mushrooms gently in cool water. Pat dry with paper towels or a clean tea towel. With your fingers, firmly grasp the stem of each mushroom and pull it out, levering it back and forth to loosen it. If the stems are too short, use a small knife to remove them.

Cut the very ends of the stems off and finely chop the stems. Set the caps on a greased baking sheet with stem holes up.

Melt 2 Tbsp. (30 mL) butter in a large skillet over medium heat. Sauté the onion and celery for 3–4 minutes, or until softened. Add the chopped mushroom stems and sauté for 5 minutes, adding a little water if the mixture gets too dry.

Remove from the heat and stir in the breadcrumbs, parsley, salt, and pepper. Set aside.

Preheat the oven to 375°F (190°C). Melt the remaining butter in a small saucepan. Brush the mushroom caps with butter, then fill each cap with stuffing, packing it in firmly.

Bake, uncovered, for 7–9 minutes, or until the caps have darkened and feel soft when you pinch them gently. Arrange on a plate and serve warm.

To make soft breadcrumbs, put fairly fresh white bread into the food processor with the grating blade, or hand-grate the bread.

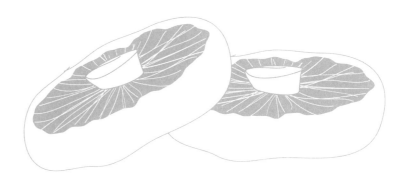

Deviled Eggs

A few months ago, I started seeing palette-like round plates in kitchen stores. After some asking around, I found out they were deviled-egg platters, coming out of a 20-year hibernation. If you see one, buy it— it makes serving these tasty little gems much more elegant.

Serves 4-6

4	eggs	4
3 Tbsp.	mayonnaise	45 mL
2 Tbsp.	minced celery	30 mL
2 tsp.	minced onion	10 mL
1/4 tsp.	mustard powder	1.2 mL
large pinch	salt	large pinch
small pinch	pepper	small pinch
	paprika for sprinkling	

To hard-boil the eggs, use a large spoon to place them carefully in a medium saucepan of gently boiling water. Simmer them gently for about 10 minutes. Run the eggs under cold water for a few minutes to cool them enough to handle. Break the shells by tapping each egg on the counter and then pulling the crushed shells off with your fingers under cold running water—they will come off easily.

Pat eggs dry with paper towel. Cut each egg in half lengthwise. Use your fingers to loosen the white from around the yolk of each half, then invert each half and let the yolk drop into a medium bowl. Arrange the whites on a serving platter.

Mash the yolks with a fork. Add the mayonnaise and mix until smooth. Add the celery, onion, mustard powder, salt, and pepper, and mix until well blended.

Heap the filling into whites using a spoon—or see the sidebar for other tips on filling. Sprinkle each egg half with a little bit of paprika.

Cover and chill 30 minutes to 1 hour before serving.

If you're serving these for a party where you want to impress people, there are two ways to make these look neater and nicer than they would if you just spooned the filling in. Number 1: empty the filling into a small resealable plastic bag. Cut the one bottom corner off, and squeeze the filling out into the eggs. Pretty! Number 2: go out and buy a piping bag and use the star-shaped end to pipe the yolk mixture into the eggs. Beautiful!

Bruschetta

This is a wonderful dish to serve as an appetizer or as a finger food at parties—although you will need to provide napkins. Don't even try to make this dish if you can't find good tomatoes. You need ripe, flavorful ones to make a good bruschetta.

Makes about 1½ dozen crostini

3	medium tomatoes (about 2 cups /500 mL), diced	3
2 Tbsp.	minced red onion	30 mL
1 Tbsp. + 4 tsp.	olive oil (approx.)	35 mL
¹/₄ tsp.	salt	1.2 mL
pinch	pepper	pinch
1 Tbsp. + 1 tsp.	fresh basil leaves, torn into small pieces	20 mL
1	baguette, sliced at an angle into ¹/₂-inch (1-cm) slices	1

In a medium bowl, mix together the tomatoes, onion, 1 Tbsp. (15 mL) olive oil, salt, pepper, and basil. Set aside.

To make the crostini, heat 1 tsp. (5 mL) olive oil in a large skillet over medium heat. Brush each side of the baguette slices with olive oil. Grill in the skillet for 4–5 minutes on each side, or until golden, adding more olive oil to the pan for the second round if you need to.

Arrange the crostini on a platter and top each slice with about 1 Tbsp. (15 mL) of bruschetta topping. Serve immediately.

Never refrigerate raw tomatoes if you can help it. They go spongy and pretty awful if you do. Whenever you're making a dish with raw tomatoes, try to estimate just enough for the number you're serving, so that you don't waste a lot.

Garlic Basil Bread

This fantastic garlic bread is really my good friend Sarah's. As she walks to work every day, she gets enough exercise to eat such delicacies on a regular basis while keeping her impossibly petite, slender frame—however, the same cannot be said for her cat Tabeatha, who also holds this recipe in very high regard.

Serves 4

1/4 cup	butter	60 mL
1/2 cup	olive oil	125 mL
1	large clove garlic, minced	1
1/3 cup	fresh basil leaves	80 mL
pinch	salt	pinch
1 loaf	crusty Italian (Calabrese) bread	1 loaf

Put the butter and olive oil into a small-to-medium saucepan. Heat over medium-low heat, stirring, until the butter is melted and has combined with the oil. Add the garlic and heat until you can smell a rich garlic aroma. Add the basil and continue to heat just until all the leaves are wilted. Stir in the salt. Remove from heat.

Use a large serrated knife to slice the bread into 1-inch (2.5-cm) slices —*but* don't slice right through the bottom. Slice almost to the bottom, but not through the crust—this will create slices that stay intact as a loaf while cooking and serving, and guests can easily pull them apart. Once the loaf is sliced, place it on a large piece of folded aluminum foil—you need it to be 2 layers thick. Fold up the sides and ends slightly so that the butter mixture doesn't dribble out.

Brush the butter mixture thoroughly between the slices of bread, coating both sides of each slice. To separate the slices enough to do this, lift the loaf, putting one hand under the slices you're brushing. Make sure you put at least one basil leaf between each slice. Brush the top and sides of the loaf as well.

Use another folded piece of aluminum foil to cover the loaf, and pinch the bottom and top pieces together so the loaf is thoroughly wrapped.

Bake in the center of a 350°F (175°C) oven for about 25 minutes or in a 325°F (165°C) oven for 35 minutes. Remove from the oven and open the foil—the bread should be hot in the center and slightly crispy on top. Serve immediately. Leftovers reheat well.

Egg Rolls

If you want translucent, light, chewy rice wraps filled with coriander and raw vegetables, go look in some other book. These are the real thing—you may remember them fondly from dinners out with your parents at the local Chinese food restaurant. You can deep-fry these if you want, but I shallow-fry them, and it works just as well. This recipe serves a crowd, but it can be halved easily.

Makes about 20 rolls

¹/₂ tsp.	cornstarch	2.5 mL
¹/₄ tsp.	freshly ground black pepper	1.2mL
1 Tbsp.	vegetarian oyster sauce	15 mL
1 tsp.	hoisin sauce	5 mL
1 Tbsp.	soy sauce	15 mL
1 Tbsp.	water	15 mL
1 Tbsp.	peanut oil	15 mL
1	large carrot, peeled and finely diced	1
1 cup	finely diced extra-firm tofu	250 mL
1 Tbsp.	minced fresh ginger	15 mL
4	cloves garlic, minced	4
1¹/₂ cups	finely shredded green cabbage	375 mL
³/₄ cup	finely diced mushrooms	185 mL
4 cups	bean sprouts, rinsed and dried	1 L
¹/₂	package egg roll wrappers (about 20)	¹/₂
	peanut or vegetable oil for frying	

In a small bowl, combine the cornstarch, pepper, vegetarian oyster sauce, hoisin sauce, soy sauce, and water until thoroughly mixed. Set aside.

Heat the peanut oil in a wok or large, deep skillet over high heat. Add the carrot, tofu, ginger, and garlic, and stir-fry over high heat for 4–5 minutes, or until the tofu and carrot have started to brown.

Add the cabbage and stir-fry for another 4–5 minutes, or until the vegetables and tofu have browned in places and look crispy.

Add the mushrooms and stir-fry for another 4–5 minutes, adding a little water if the mixture gets too dry.

Add the bean sprouts and stir-fry for 5 minutes, or until they've softened slightly.

Add the sauce and toss to coat for about 1 minute. Remove from the heat and let cool—the filling doesn't need to cool completely, but should be no warmer than lukewarm when it's put into the wrappers.

On a clean, dry surface, stack your egg roll wrappers on one side, and put a small bowl of water on the other. Put 1 egg roll wrapper in the center. Put about 2 Tbsp. (30 mL) filling onto the wrapper, spreading it along half of the wrapper lengthwise. Leave about $1/2$ inch (1.2 cm) of space at the ends, as you'll need to seal them.

With your finger, moisten all around the edges of the wrapper with water. Fold the wrapper over the filling and pinch it shut all around, using a little more water if you need to make it stick.

Repeat this with as many wrappers as you want egg rolls.

Pour about 1 inch (2.5 cm) oil into a deep skillet. Heat on medium-high until a tiny piece of egg roll wrapper sizzles and bubbles when it's dropped in.

Put 3 or 4 egg rolls into the oil—don't put in more, because you need enough time to turn them all properly without burning them. Let them fry for about 3 minutes, or until the bottom is golden brown and bubbly. Using tongs, turn them over and fry the other side. If necessary, hold them with the ends in the oil for a moment to crisp up. When cooked evenly, remove and place on paper towel to drain, then transfer to a baking sheet in a 250°F (120°C) oven. Repeat with all the egg rolls, adding more oil if necessary.

Serve hot with Peanut Sauce (p. 79) or plum sauce with a little hoisin mixed in.

If you have leftover egg roll wrappers, save them to make Sweet Potato Ravioli (p.108).

Meatless Meatballs

These low-fat beauties must be tasted to be believed. Serve as an appetizer with mustard for dipping, or with Spaghetti with Tomato Sauce and Herbed Mushrooms (p. 96).

Makes 20-25 balls

2 cups	TVP granules	500 mL
2 tsp.	chili powder	10 mL
1 tsp.	garlic powder	5 mL
1/2 tsp.	salt	2.5 mL
3 Tbsp.	ketchup	45 mL
1 3/4 cups	very hot vegetable stock	435 mL
1	medium onion, minced	1
1 Tbsp.	olive oil	15 mL
1/2 cup	unbleached flour	125 mL

Preheat the oven to 350°F (175°C). Mix the TVP, chili powder, garlic powder, salt, and ketchup in a large bowl. Add the stock and stir well. Let sit, stirring once or twice.

Sauté the onion in olive oil on medium heat for 6–7 minutes, or until soft. Add the onion to the TVP mixture. Add the flour and stir thoroughly.

Shape into 1 1/2-inch (4-cm) balls and place on a non-stick cookie sheet. Bake for approximately 20 minutes, until slightly browned.

Spicy Black Beans

Eat this Mexican-inspired food wrapped in flour tortillas with sour cream, chopped tomatoes, lettuce, grated cheddar, and Guacamole (p. 77).

Serves 4-6

1 Tbsp.	olive oil	15 mL
1	medium onion, chopped	1
2	cloves garlic, crushed	2
4 tsp.	ground cumin	20 mL
pinch	cayenne	pinch
2	19-oz. (540-mL) cans black beans	2
1 cup	corn kernels	250 mL
1/4 tsp.	salt	1.2 mL

Heat the olive oil over medium heat in a large skillet. Add the onion and garlic and sauté for 6–8 minutes, or until softened. Add the cumin and cayenne and sauté for about a minute to coat the onions thoroughly.

Drain about 2 Tbsp. (30 mL) liquid from each can of black beans. Add the beans with their remaining liquid to the onions, and let simmer, stirring occasionally, for about 8 minutes, or until there's very little liquid left.

Add the corn kernels and salt, and let simmer for another 3–4 minutes.

Not-Refried Beans

I have Ilana Weitzman to thank for this simple recipe that is a bit sneaky—as the title indicates, the beans aren't actually refried. These are excellent spread on a tortilla with Guacamole (p. 77), fresh lettuce, sautéed onions, and tomato.

Serves 4

1	19-oz. (540-mL) can kidney beans	1
1 Tbsp.	olive oil	15 mL
1	large clove garlic, crushed	1
1 1/2 tsp.	ground cumin	7.5 mL
1/4 tsp.	ground cinnamon	1.2 mL
1/4 tsp.	salt	1.2 mL

Open the can of beans and drain off about 1/4 inch (.5 cm) of the liquid. Set aside.

Heat the oil in a large skillet over medium heat. Sauté the garlic for about a minute—don't let it brown.

Empty the beans with their liquid into the skillet and stir. Simmer, stirring occasionally, for about 5 minutes, or until some of the liquid has reduced. Stir in the cumin, cinnamon, and salt, and remove from the heat.

Empty the mixture into a blender or food processor and blend until smooth, turning the blender off and scraping often. If you're having trouble getting the beans to blend, add a tablespoon or two (15–30 mL) of water until the beans incorporate into a smooth purée.

If you're using a blender for these beans, you will find that they will make your blender impossible to clean if you don't do something about it right away. Use this great tip for cleaning blenders that I learned from the queen of homekeeping, Heloise Cruse: put a few drops of dishwashing liquid into the blender, and half-fill it with warm water. Put the lid on and "blend" this mixture for a minute or so. If this doesn't completely clean the blender, just repeat until it does.

Baked Beans

This recipe combines my Brit tendencies—to slather these things over toast, baked potatoes, and eggs—with my Canadian upbringing: they're studded with maple syrup and molasses. Although this recipe is not as much work as you would expect, you need to soak the beans beforehand. The baked beans freeze well in airtight containers.

Serves 6

2 cups	dry white beans	500 mL
1 Tbsp.	olive oil	15 mL
1	medium onion, finely chopped	1
3	cloves garlic, crushed	3
1/4 cup	molasses	60 mL
1/4 cup	ketchup	60 mL
2 1/2 tsp.	Dijon mustard	12.5 mL
2 Tbsp.	maple syrup	30 mL
1/2 tsp.	salt	2.5 mL
pinch	pepper	pinch

Sort through the dry beans, picking out any that look odd or discolored. Rinse them in a colander under cold running water, and transfer to a large bowl. Cover with at least 3 inches (8 cm) of cold water. Soak for at least 4 hours, but preferably overnight.

Rinse the beans and put them in a large saucepan with plenty of water. Boil gently until soft. This will take anywhere from 35–55 minutes, depending on how long you soaked them. Drain the beans over a medium bowl to reserve the cooking water. Set aside.

Heat the oil in a skillet over medium heat. Add the onion and garlic and sauté until soft. Set aside. Preheat the oven to 350°F (175°C). Put the beans into a large ovenproof dish. Add all remaining ingredients, as well as 1 1/2 cups (375 mL) of bean liquid. Stir.

Cover and bake, removing from the oven and stirring every 20 minutes or so, until most of the liquid has been absorbed and the sauce is thick, about 1 1/2 hours. Add more salt and pepper to taste if desired.

Dry white beans are sometimes called navy beans or "pigeon peas," though I have no idea what those are. Basically, if they're small and white, you've got the right ones.

Onion Fried Rice

This old-style side dish, which is great for using up leftover rice, often finds itself sitting in as a main course for me. To turn this into vegetable fried rice, simply add julienned carrots, frozen peas, or whatever else you like to the onions and stir-fry together. You can also add chickpeas, black beans, or finely diced firm tofu for some protein.

Serves 4–6

1 Tbsp.	peanut oil	15 mL
4	medium onions, chopped	4
1/2 cup	onion soup, made from onion soup mix	125 mL
4 Tbsp.	soy sauce	60 mL
2 tsp.	hoisin sauce	10 mL
1/4 tsp.	Korean chili paste	1.2 mL
4 cups	cooked white or brown rice	1 L
1/4 tsp.	sesame oil (optional)	1.2 mL

Heat the peanut oil in a wok or deep skillet over medium-high heat. Add the onions and stir-fry, stirring often, for 7–9 minutes, or until softened and browned. If the onions become too dry, add 1 Tbsp. (15 mL) onion soup.

Add the soy sauce and coat the onions evenly. Add the hoisin, remaining onion soup, and chili paste, and stir to combine. Add the rice and stir-fry for 4–5 minutes, stirring very often, or until the rice is heated through. If you want, add sesame oil just before serving.

Spanish Rice

I don't know what is actually Spanish about this rice, but I do know that the recipe is faithful to the '60s classic of the same name. This zesty, delicious rice is fantastic in a burrito with Spicy Black Beans (p.150), and also makes an excellent and nutritious main dish on its own.

Serves 6

1	28-oz. (796-mL) can tomatoes	1
1 Tbsp.	olive oil	15 mL
1	large stalk celery, diced	1
1	large onion, chopped	1
1	large green pepper, chopped	1
3	cloves garlic, minced	3
1 1/4 tsp.	salt	6.2 mL
2 1/4 tsp.	chili powder	12 mL
1 tsp.	oregano	5 mL
pinch	chili flakes	pinch
4 cups	cooked white or brown rice	1 L

Empty the tomatoes, with the liquid from the can, into a medium bowl and use a potato masher to mash them into smaller pieces. Set aside.

Heat the olive oil in a wok or large, deep skillet over medium-high heat. Add the celery, onion, green pepper, and garlic, and sauté for 3–4 minutes, then add 1/2 tsp. (2.5 mL) salt. Sauté for another 3–4 minutes, or until the vegetables have softened slightly.

Add the chili powder, oregano, and chili flakes, and sauté for 1–2 minutes to coat the vegetables thoroughly. Add the tomatoes, reduce the heat to medium, and simmer, uncovered, for about 20 minutes.

Add the rice and remaining salt and sauté for 5–7 minutes, or until most of the tomato liquid has been absorbed.

Rice and Mushroom Casserole

There is something extremely comforting about a casserole. This one works equally well as a side dish or main dish, and the mushrooms rise to the top prettily. Great for potlucks if you're ever dragged to one!

Serves 4–6

1 Tbsp.	olive oil	15 mL
1	medium onion, diced	1
4	cloves garlic, crushed	4
2	stalks celery, diced	2
3 cups	sliced mushrooms	750 mL
1/4 cup	nutritional yeast flakes	60 mL
1/4 tsp.	salt	1.2 mL
dash	pepper	dash
1 1/2 cups	parboiled rice, uncooked	375 mL
4 cups	onion soup, made from onion soup mix	1 L

Preheat the oven to 350°F (175°C). Heat the olive oil in a skillet over medium heat. Sauté the onion, garlic, and celery for 4–5 minutes, then add the mushrooms and sauté for 5–7 minutes, or until the mushrooms are cooked through.

Reduce the heat to low and add the yeast, salt, and pepper, stirring to coat. Add the rice and stir to coat.

Spoon the rice mixture into a 2-quart (1.8-L) baking dish. Pour the onion soup over top and stir.

Cover and bake for 45–55 minutes, or until the liquid is absorbed. Let sit, uncovered, for 5 minutes before serving.

Onion soup mix is a great substitute for vegetable stock when you want a change. You can find it in bulk at your health food or bulk store. Make sure it's vegetarian—sometimes it will contain beef fat. Experiment to see how much stock powder is needed per cup (250 mL) of hot water. It can range from a teaspoon (5 mL) to a tablespoon (15 mL). For this recipe, add an extra cup's (250 mL) worth of powder to give the rice more flavor.

Corn Fritters

My dad used to serve these with his Mixed Grill dinners, consisting of a lot of meat, some crispy french fries, and some dark fried onions. I'll still go in for the fries and onions, but I would substitute The Colonel's Tofu (p. 144) for the meat. These fritters taste great with spicy salsa, and they're equally good slathered with Golden Mushroom Gravy (p. 82).

Serves 4–6

1	egg	1
1/4 cup	milk	60 mL
1/4 cup	cold water	60 mL
1/2 cup	flour	125 mL
1/4 tsp.	baking powder	1.2 mL
1/2 tsp.	salt	2.5 mL
1 1/2 cups	fresh or frozen corn kernels, or one 12-oz. (340-mL) can of corn kernels, drained	375 mL
3 Tbsp.	chopped fresh parsley	45 mL
large pinch	pepper	large pinch
3 tsp.	butter (approx.)	15 mL

Beat the egg lightly (15–30 seconds) in a small bowl. Stir in the milk and water. Set aside.

In a medium bowl, combine the flour, baking powder, and salt. Form a well in the middle. Pour the egg mixture into the well and stir to combine until it isn't very lumpy—a few lumps are all right. Add the corn, parsley, and pepper.

Heat about 1 tsp. (5 mL) butter in a large skillet over medium-high heat. Drop 2 Tbsp. (30 mL) batter onto the skillet for each fritter. Fry for about 4 minutes on each side, or until browned and crispy. As you fry each round of fritters, add more butter to the skillet.

These fritters are unbelievably good if you use fresh corn. Here's how to remove kernels from the cob. First, remove the husks and cornsilk. For 1 1/2 cups (375 mL) corn, you'll need about 3 cobs. Blanch the corn by putting the cobs into boiling water for 2 minutes. Hold each cob upright in a bowl, and use a sharp knife to cut the kernels off the cob in a downward motion. Rotate the cob until you've cut off all the kernels.

Yorkshire Pudding

For a long time, I regarded this delightful side dish as belonging solely to childhood; my dad would make miniature Yorkshire Puddings in muffin cups whenever he made a roast beef. But then I picked up an old cheeseboard at a Salvation Army sale that described in detail an "Olde English Beefeater Dinner." And there the pudding was, nestled between the roast beef and the apple pie with cream. This is best with Golden Mushroom Gravy (p. 82).

Serves 4–6

1¼ cups	flour	300 mL
½ tsp.	baking powder	2.5 mL
½ tsp.	salt	2.5 mL
2	eggs	2
1¼ cups	milk	300 mL
	butter	

Preheat the oven to 375°F (190°C). In a medium bowl, sift together the flour, baking powder, and salt. Set aside.

In a large bowl, beat the eggs with an electric mixer on high speed for about 1 minute. Add the milk and beat for about 30 seconds more. Gradually beat in the flour mixture, and keep beating until smooth.

Grease 12 muffin cups liberally with butter, then pour the batter into each cup until it is almost full.

Bake for 12–15 minutes, or until the puddings have risen dramatically and are brown around the edges. Let cool for a minute or so, then use a butter knife to loosen and remove the puddings. Serve immediately.

desserts

Lemon Meringue Pie

If you've never made a lemon meringue pie before, you really should. It's pretty hard to mess up, and you'll be so proud of yourself when your guests shower you with compliments. And believe me, they will— the truth is, almost no one makes pies from scratch anymore, let alone a real classic like lemon meringue.

Makes one 9-inch (23-cm) pie

1/2 batch	Sweet Pastry (p. 27)	1/2 batch
1 cup	dried beans	250 mL
1 1/4 cups + 6 Tbsp.	sugar	390 mL
dash	salt	dash
3 Tbsp.	cornstarch	45 mL
3 Tbsp.	all-purpose flour	45 mL
1 1/2 cups	hot water	375 mL
3	egg yolks, slightly beaten	3
2 Tbsp.	butter	30 mL
1 tsp.	finely grated lemon rind	5 mL
1/3 cup	lemon juice	80 mL
3	egg whites	3
1/2 tsp.	vanilla	2.5 mL
1/4 tsp.	cream of tartar	1.2 mL

First, prebake your pie crust. Preheat the oven to 400°F (200°C), then roll out your pastry to fit your pie plate, using the pastry tips from p. 28. Fold the pastry over your rolling pin, lift over the pie plate, and press it down into the plate. Using scissors, trim the outside to 1/4 inch (.5 cm) larger than the rim of the plate. Use your thumb to flute the edge, pressing down against the rim of the plate. Cut a piece of wax paper into a circle to place in the bottom of the pie crust. Place the dried beans on the wax paper to prevent the crust from bubbling up while cooking. When you're done with this crust, you can save these beans in a jar as your "pie weights" and reuse them forever. Bake for about 10 minutes, or until the pastry is golden; lift up the beans and wax paper to check. Set aside to cool. Turn the oven down to 350°F (175°C).

In a medium saucepan, mix together 1¼ cups (300 mL) sugar, the salt, cornstarch, and flour. Gradually add the hot water, stirring constantly. Heat, stirring frequently, over medium heat until the mixture starts to bubble. If any lumps form, use a whisk. Let it come to the boil, then reduce the heat and cook, stirring, for 2–3 minutes. Whisk about 2 Tbsp. (30 mL) of this mixture into the egg yolks, and then pour this back into the saucepan. Bring it to a boil, stirring constantly, and cook for 2 minutes. Add the butter and lemon rind, stirring well. Remove from the heat and gradually add the lemon juice, stirring constantly.

Pour this into your pastry shell, smoothing with a rubber spatula. Set aside.

Beat the egg whites, vanilla, and cream of tartar in a large bowl at medium speed for 4–5 minutes, or until soft peaks form. To test for soft peaks, turn off your electric beaters and pull the beaters up. If peaks form but the tops fold down, that's right. Beat in the 6 Tbsp. (90 mL) sugar, 1 Tbsp. (15 mL) at a time. Beat at medium speed until stiff peaks form, 6–8 minutes. The tops of stiff peaks won't fold over at all.

Spread the meringue over the pie with a rubber spatula. It's okay if the lemon mixture is still warm; in fact, this is preferable. Push the meringue right out to the junction of the lemon filling and the pastry to "seal" the meringue—this will prevent the meringue from shrinking. Lift up with your spatula to form peaks in the meringue.

Bake for 12–15 minutes, or until the meringue is well tinged with brown on top. Let cool before serving.

Here are some lemon tips: first wash the lemons that you're going to use for the rind. Rind the lemons before you juice them! To get the most juice out of your lemons, roll them around on the counter, pressing down with the heel of your hand. This will make it much easier to juice the lemons and it will yield up to ¼ cup (60 mL) extra juice.

Vanilla Cream Topping

This topping can be as decadent or as virtuous as you like, as you can use full-fat sour cream, fat-free yogurt, or anything in between. Use this topping on hot or cold desserts, on pancakes, or as a dip for fruit. Leftovers make excellent smoothies with fruit and milk or soymilk.

Serves 4–6

1 cup	sour cream or unflavored yogurt	250 mL
3 Tbsp.	maple syrup	45 mL
1¹/₂ tsp.	vanilla extract	7.5 mL

Combine all ingredients in a small bowl.

Raspberry Sauce

I made this sauce expressly to crown the Vegan Chocolate-Rum Cheesecake on p.182, but it is equally good on Rice Pudding (p.191). More *au courant* people would call it a "coulis." You can use this basic formula to experiment with different types of fruits, from strawberries to mangos. Just be conservative with the sugar at first, and then add more to taste.

Makes about 1 cup (250 mL)

1 cup	unsweetened raspberries	250 mL
1 cup	water	250 mL
¹/₄ cup + 2 Tbsp.	sugar	90 mL
2 tsp.	cornstarch	10 mL
¹/₂ tsp.	grated lemon rind	2.5 mL

Put all ingredients into a food processor or blender and purée until smooth.

Transfer to a small saucepan and bring to a boil. Let boil for about 1 minute, then reduce the heat and simmer for 3–5 minutes, or until the sauce has darkened in color and thickened.

Pour the sauce through a fine sieve with a bowl underneath to strain out seeds.

Hello Dolly Squares

These easy-to-make squares were a staple of the '70s, and I say it's high time for a comeback. Perfect for your next bake sale, animal-rights meeting, or Barbra Streisand video night (I don't know if these squares were named after the 1969 musical, but they're a wild ride, just like a Barbra film!). Make sure you use unsweetened coconut.

Makes 24 squares

¹/₂ cup	butter	125 mL
1¹/₄ cups	graham wafer crumbs	300 mL
1¹/₂ cups	semisweet chocolate chips	375 mL
1¹/₂ cups	unsweetened coconut	375 mL
¹/₂ cup	walnuts or pecans, chopped	125 mL
1¹/₂ cups	sweetened condensed milk	375 mL

Preheat the oven to 350°F (175°C). Place the butter in a 9- x 13- inch (23- x 33-cm) baking pan and melt in the oven.

Remove from the oven, mix the crumbs in, and spread evenly in the pan. Sprinkle the chocolate chips over top in an even layer, followed by the coconut, then the nuts. Pour the milk evenly over this, spreading with a rubber spatula or knife until it's even.

Bake for about 35 minutes, or until the milky layer isn't liquid anymore. It should be slightly golden. Let cool partially in the pan, and cut into squares before completely cool. Remove from the pan when cool.

Blondie Bars

These butterscotch brownies are dense, chewy, and addictive—especially with a good cup of tea. They're also extremely easy to make.

Makes 32 bars

1 cup	butter, melted	250 mL
2 cups	brown sugar, packed	500 mL
2	eggs	2
2 tsp.	vanilla	10 mL
2 Tbsp.	milk	30 mL
1 cup	chopped walnuts, or ¹/₂ cup (125 mL) each chopped walnuts and chocolate or butterscotch chips	250 mL
1¹/₃ cups	all-purpose flour	330 mL
2 tsp.	baking powder	10 mL
1 tsp.	salt	5 mL

Preheat the oven to 350°F (175°C). In a large bowl, mix together the butter and sugar. Beat the eggs in one at a time. Beat in the vanilla and milk. Stir in the walnuts and chocolate chips, if using. Set aside.

Sift together the flour, baking powder, and salt in a medium bowl. Add to the butter mixture and stir to combine—don't overmix.

Turn into a greased 9- x 13-inch (23- x 33-cm) baking dish and bake for 30–35 minutes, or until golden brown. Let cool for 5–7 minutes in the pan; cut into bars while still warm.

Homestyle Apple Pie

Real estate agents know that an apple pie baking in the oven creates the best possible ambience at an open house. When you make an apple pie from scratch, it's easy to see why: the aroma it creates is heavenly. This recipe is good and simple, but that's all you need. You can also use this as a base if you would like to combine the apples with berries.

Makes one 9-inch (23-cm) pie

6 cups	tart, crispy apples, peeled, cored, and sliced (about 6 large apples)	1.5 L
1 tsp.	lemon juice	5 mL
1/2 tsp.	vanilla	2.5 mL
2/3 cup	sugar	160 mL
1 Tbsp.	all-purpose flour	15 mL
1/2–3/4 tsp.	cinnamon	2.5–4 mL
pinch	nutmeg	pinch
pinch	salt	pinch
2 Tbsp.	butter	30 mL
1 batch	Sweet Pastry (p. 27)	1 batch
2 Tbsp.	milk (approx.)	30 mL

Combine the apples, lemon juice, and vanilla in a large bowl. Set aside.

In a small bowl, combine the sugar, flour, cinnamon, nutmeg, and salt. Add to the apple mixture and mix in thoroughly.

Prepare your pie shell, using the pastry tips from p. 28 as a guide.

Preheat the oven to 375°F (190°C). Spread the apple mixture into your pie shell. Dab the butter on top. Top with the second layer of pastry. Brush the top with milk. With a knife, cut small slits in the top of the pie to let air escape.

Bake for 45–60 minutes, or until the pastry is golden brown.

Banana Cream Pie

A good vegan margarine works well in this recipe for all you purists out there, but I won't suggest non-vegans use real whipped cream rather than whipped topping. "Edible oil product" may be vile on its own, but there's something sumptuous and trashy about it in this recipe.

Makes one 9-inch (23-cm) pie

1¼ cups	graham cracker crumbs	300 mL
⅓ cup	butter, melted	80 mL
2 Tbsp.	brown sugar, lightly packed	30 mL
4	ripe bananas, sliced	4
3 cups	whipped topping	750 mL
¼ cup	maple syrup	60 mL
1½ tsp.	vanilla	7.5 mL
2 Tbsp.	grated chocolate	30 mL

Preheat the oven to 350°F (175°C). In a medium bowl, mix together graham crumbs, butter, and brown sugar. Press evenly into a buttered 9-inch (23-cm) pie plate. Bake for about 5 minutes, just to let the crust set. Let cool.

Put 2 sliced bananas, whipped topping, 2 Tbsp. (30 mL) of the maple syrup, and 1 tsp. (5 mL) vanilla into a blender or food processor, and purée until smooth (about a minute), scraping down the sides halfway through.

In a small bowl, combine the remaining bananas, maple syrup, and vanilla. Spread the bananas out evenly in the bottom and sides of the cooled crust, drizzling any remaining syrup over top.

Spoon the cream filling into the crust, using a knife or rubber spatula to spread out evenly. Make sure that all the banana slices are covered; otherwise they'll discolor. Garnish with grated chocolate. Chill for at least an hour before serving.

Ranger Cookies

I used to read a lot of books from the '70s on cookie-making. I remember one recipe for Ranger Cookies that consisted of a basic cookie dough with raisins, nuts, and rice crisps. A few years later I tried it, using a basic buttery cookie dough, leaving out the stuff I didn't like (raisins and nuts), and adding what I did like (chocolate chips).

Makes about 4 dozen cookies
(if you don't eat any dough first, which is nearly impossible)

³/₄ cup	butter, softened	80 mL
1¹/₄ cups	brown sugar, lightly packed	300 mL
¹/₄ cup	white sugar	60 mL
2	eggs	2
1 tsp.	vanilla	5 mL
2 cups	all-purpose flour	500 mL
1 tsp.	baking soda	5 mL
1 tsp.	salt	5 mL
1 cup	semisweet chocolate chips	250 mL
1 cup	rice crisp cereal	250 mL

In a large bowl, cream the butter and sugars together. Beat in the eggs one at a time, adding the vanilla with the second egg. In a medium-size bowl, combine flour with baking soda and salt. Gradually add the dry ingredients to the wet ingredients. Add the chocolate chips and rice crisps.

Preheat the oven to 350°F (175°C). Drop by tablespoonfuls about 2–3 inches (5–7.5 cm) apart on a non-stick cookie sheet, or a cookie sheet lined with parchment paper.

Bake for 9–11 minutes, or until the cookies are golden brown. Let them cool on the cookie sheet for a minute before you transfer them onto a cooling rack.

There is one vital trick to these cookies: *do not* let the dough sit! Start putting batches in the oven as soon as the dough is made. In high school, a friend called with some hilarious, long, convoluted story right before I put these cookies in the oven, and I let the dough sit for about an hour. I wound up with soggy, chewy rice crisps that ruined the cookies, though I did have some great dirt on a friend's vile ex.

Snowball Cookies

I usually make these cookies at Christmas because they're so much easier than fiddling around with decorations and icing. One tip: don't taste the shortbread dough. It won't taste sweet enough. Instead, wait until you have tossed the warm cookies in icing sugar—and then see if you can stop yourself!

Makes about 3 dozen cookies

1 cup	butter, softened	250 mL
2 tsp.	vanilla	10 mL
1 Tbsp.	milk	15 mL
$1/4$ cup + 1 cup	icing sugar (approx.)	300 mL
2 cups	all-purpose flour	500 mL
$1/4$ tsp.	salt	1.2 mL

Cream the butter in a large bowl. Add the vanilla, milk, and $1/4$ cup (60 mL) icing sugar, and cream together. Sift in the flour and salt and combine well. The dough will be more like pastry dough than cookie dough.

Preheat the oven to 350°F (175°C). Roll into balls about 1 inch (2.5 cm) in diameter. Place on an ungreased cookie sheet. You can place them close together; they don't expand much.

Bake for about 20 minutes. Cool for 2 minutes or so, and then, while still warm, shake about 4 cookies at a time in a paper bag with about $1/2$ cup (125 mL) of the icing sugar. Remove from the bag and place on wire racks to cool.

Repeat with all the cookies, adding more icing sugar as you need it. This will create a "snowy" coating.

Apple-Raspberry Crumble

You may know this dessert as "cobbler." The crumble topping lends itself well to most other fruits, such as peaches, blueberries, blackberries, and pears. Serve this warm with vanilla ice cream, whipped cream, or evaporated milk .

Serves 6–8

1 1/2 cups	all-purpose flour	375 mL
3/4 cup	quick-cooking rolled oats	185 mL
1/4 tsp.	salt	1.2 mL
1/2 cup	brown sugar	125 mL
2 Tbsp. + 1/4 cup	white sugar	90 mL
2/3 cup	butter, cubed	160 mL
2 tsp.	vanilla extract	10 mL
3 Tbsp.	milk	45 mL
5	apples, peeled and sliced	5
2 cups	unsweetened raspberries	500 mL

In a medium bowl, combine the flour, oats, salt, brown sugar, and 2 Tbsp. (30 mL) white sugar. Work the butter into the flour mixture with a pastry blender or your hands until the butter is in very small pebbles. Then add 1 tsp. (5 mL) of the vanilla, as well as the milk. Continue to work the mixture with your hands until it is holding together in a large-pebble sort of way. Set aside.

Preheat the oven to 350°F (175°C). Spread the apples evenly in a 2-quart (1.8-L) baking dish. Spread the raspberries evenly over top. Sprinkle the remaining 1/4 cup (60 mL) white sugar evenly over, as well as the remaining 1 tsp. (5 mL) vanilla.

Spread the crumble topping evenly over the fruit. Bake, uncovered, for 45 minutes, or until the crumble is brown on top.

This crumble is sweet, but not tooth-achingly so; if you like it really sweet, go ahead and add more white sugar to the topping. If you are using raspberries in syrup, drain them and cut the sugar in the fruit by a couple of tablespoons.

Apple Pudding

This may sound humble, but it's fantastic-tasting. In true British fashion, this is not really a "pudding" as you may know it—in Britain, all desserts are called "pudding." The best apples to use for this are tart, crispy apples, such as Macintosh or Granny Smith. This dessert tastes best warm with ice cream or whipped cream.

Serves 6

4 cups	apples, peeled and sliced	1 L
1/2 tsp.	ground cinnamon	2.5 mL
1/4 tsp.	ground nutmeg	1.2 mL
2 Tbsp. + 1 cup	white sugar	280 mL
1/4 cup	hot water	60 mL
2 Tbsp. + 1 cup	butter, melted	90 mL
2	eggs	2
1 tsp.	vanilla	5 mL
2/3 cup	flour	160 mL
2 tsp.	baking powder	10 mL
1/2 tsp.	salt	2.5 mL

Preheat the oven to 350°F (175°C). Butter a 9- x 11-inch (23- x 28-cm) dish. Spread the sliced apples in the bottom of the dish.

In a small bowl, mix together the cinnamon, nutmeg, and 2 Tbsp. (30 mL) sugar. Sprinkle this on top of the apples. Pour the hot water and 2 Tbsp. (30 mL) butter on top. Set aside. In a medium bowl, beat the eggs. Beat in the remaining cup (250 mL) of sugar, then the remaining 1/4 cup (60 mL) butter and the vanilla.

In a small bowl, combine the flour, baking powder, and salt. Fold into the egg mixture. Beat just until combined, and spread over the apples. Bake for about 40 minutes, or until the top is brown.

If you have the inclination, freshly grate your nutmeg. It tastes fresher than preground, and it's better than incense to perfume a room. The whole "nuts" can be bought at a bulk food store. Use the thinnest setting of your cheese grater and grate.

Rhubarb Upside-Down Cake

I have my mom to thank for this delicious way to use rhubarb. You can use fresh or frozen rhubarb, but make sure it's not in syrup. The batter will seem extremely thick, but don't worry—as the rhubarb cooks, it liquifies the batter, and it all bakes together into a heavenly cake that is especially nice warm with vanilla ice cream.

Makes one 9-inch (23-cm) square cake

1/2 cup	butter, softened	125 mL
1 cup	brown sugar	250 mL
4–5 cups	rhubarb, cut into 1/2-inch (1.2-cm) pieces	1–1.25 L
1 cup	white sugar	250 mL
1 1/2 cups	flour	375 mL
2 tsp.	baking powder	10 mL
1/2 tsp.	salt	2.5 mL
1	egg	1
1 tsp.	vanilla	5 mL
2/3 cup	milk (approx.)	160 mL

Preheat the oven to 350°F (175°C). Melt 1/4 cup (60mL) of the butter in a 9-inch (23-cm) square baking dish in the oven. Add the brown sugar and rhubarb and mix together, spreading evenly in the bottom of the pan. Set aside.

In a large bowl, sift together the white sugar, flour, baking powder, and salt. Add the remaining butter and mix into the flour mixture. The easiest way to do this is to take two butter knives and cut the butter into the flour, making crisscross motions.

In a cup measure (250-mL), beat the egg and stir in the vanilla. Fill the cup to the top with milk, mixing together.

Pour the milk mixture over the flour mixture and blend until smooth. Spread the batter evenly over the rhubarb. Bake at 350°F (175°C) for 30–40 minutes, or until a knife inserted in the center comes out clean. (Make sure to just insert it into the top "cake" layer—the rhubarb at the bottom will be moist.)

To serve, leave in the pan and cut square servings. Lift each piece out of the pan and turn it over on the plate so the rhubarb is on top.

Banana Cake with Lemon Glaze

I have never liked banana bread, and have never understood why others do. However, I do understand that desperate, frugal urge to salvage the bananas in the fruit bowl that are rapidly going over the hill. This recipe satisfies that urge beautifully and with relatively little fat. I have friends who literally squeal with delight when I make this cake.

Makes one 8-inch (20-cm) cake

2 cups	all-purpose flour	500 mL
1 tsp.	salt	5 mL
3 tsp.	baking powder	15 mL
1/4 cup	butter, at room temperature	60 mL
1/4 cup	milk	60 mL
1 cup	brown sugar	250 mL
2	eggs	2
1	lemon, rind grated, with juice of 1/2 lemon set aside	1
4	very ripe bananas, mashed	4
3/4–1 cup	icing sugar	185–250 mL

Preheat the oven to 350°F (175°C). Grease an 8-inch (20-cm) round cake pan and line the bottom with parchment paper. To do this, trace the bottom of the cake pan onto the parchment paper and cut out.

In a medium bowl, mix together the flour, salt, and baking powder. Set aside.

With an electric mixer or a strong arm, beat the butter, milk, and sugar until well blended. Beat in the eggs one at a time, adding about 2 Tbsp. (30 mL) of the flour mixture with the second egg. Beat in the lemon rind, and fold in the rest of the flour mixture and the mashed bananas.

Turn into the cake pan and bake for about 1 hour, or until a toothpick inserted in the center comes out clean. Remove immediately from the pan and let sit on a cooling rack.

While the cake cools, make the glaze. Squeeze the juice of half a lemon into a small bowl, and gradually add enough icing sugar to form a thick glaze that will pour slowly. This should be about 3/4 cup (185 mL), but you may wish to adjust it to taste.

When the cake is cool, pour the glaze on top and spread it evenly. Some of it should run down the sides nicely.

Chocolate Sour Cream Cake

Have you ever heard older members of your family rave on about cakes that "taste better the next day"? Well, prepare to enter the secret society! Sour cream cakes, as a rule, become denser and richer after a day or two, and they stay moist forever if they're kept in a covered cake dish. Here I've modernized this '60s tradition.

Makes *two 8-inch (20-cm) layers*

6 squares	semisweet chocolate	6 squares
1/2 cup	butter, at room temperature	125 mL
1 1/4 cups	white sugar	300 mL
1 tsp.	vanilla	5 mL
2	eggs	2
1 cup	hot water	250 mL
2 cups	all-purpose flour	500 mL
1 tsp.	baking soda	5 mL
1/2 tsp.	salt	2.5 mL
3/4 cup	light sour cream	185 mL

Melt the chocolate in a double boiler, or in a glass or metal bowl set over a saucepan of simmering water. ***Don't let the bowl touch the water; otherwise the chocolate will scorch***. Set aside and let cool.

Grease and flour two 8-inch (20-cm) round cake pans. Line the bottoms with parchment paper. To do this, trace the bottom of the cake pan onto the parchment paper and cut out. Set aside.

In a large bowl, beat together the butter and sugar until fluffy. Beat in the vanilla. Beat in the eggs one at a time, then beat in 2/3 cup (160 mL) hot water.

In a medium bowl, sift together the flour, baking soda, and salt.

Add about $^1/_3$ of the flour mixture to the butter mixture and beat in. Then add about $^1/_3$ of the sour cream and beat in. Continue to add flour and sour cream alternately until all are combined. Add the cooled chocolate and remaining $^1/_3$ cup (80 mL) of hot water, and beat just until combined.

Preheat the oven to 350°F (175°C). Transfer half the batter to each cake pan, and bake on the center oven rack for 30–35 minutes, or until a chopstick or other wooden stick inserted in the center comes out clean.

Let cool in the pans for 3–4 minutes, then run a knife around the edge of the cakes to loosen. Carefully turn onto cooling racks and lift the pans off. Remove the parchment paper and let cool. Frost with Coconut Penuche Frosting (p. 174).

Coconut Penuche Frosting

"Penuche" is Mexican Spanish for a fudge made with brown sugar, butter, and cream or milk. This frosting deserves its name, made even more rich with the addition of coconut. It is dense, and you need to work quickly with it—make it when your cake is just about cool, and frost the cake as soon as it is ready.

Frosts two 8-inch (20-cm) layers

$^1/_3$ cup	butter	80 mL
1 cup	brown sugar, firmly packed	250 mL
2 Tbsp. + $^1/_4$ cup	milk	90 mL
1 cup	unsweetened coconut	250 mL
$2^1/_2$–3 cups	icing sugar	625–750 mL

Melt the butter in a small saucepan over medium heat. Add brown sugar and 2 Tbsp. (30 mL) milk, and heat until simmering, stirring very often. Let simmer for about 2 minutes, stirring constantly. Remove from the heat and transfer to a mixing bowl. Let cool for about 5 minutes.

Heat the remaining $^1/_4$ cup (60 mL) milk, but not to boiling. Add the hot milk and coconut to the butter mixture and stir well to combine. Gradually add the icing sugar, stirring very well, until the icing is spreadable, but not too thick—the frosting will thicken as it continues to cool.

Use immediately. When frosting two 8-inch (20-cm) layers, spread a generous layer on the middle and top, but don't frost the sides. You don't want to overdo it with this icing!

Last-Minute Fruit Salad

This recipe responds well to variations not only in fruit, but in liqueur, making it a perfectly elegant throw-together dessert. Good fruit substitutions include watermelon, banana, and fresh berries. Instead of Grand Marnier, try Drambuie or Amaretto.

Serves 4

1	large crispy apple, peeled and cored	1
1	seedless orange, peeled, with all pith removed	1
1	ripe pear, cored	1
$1/2$	cantaloupe or honeydew melon, peeled with seeds scooped out	$1/2$
$3/4$ cup	seedless red or green grapes, washed	185 mL
3 Tbsp.	lemon or lime juice	45 mL
3 Tbsp.	Grand Marnier	45 mL
$1/2$ tsp.	cinnamon	2.5 mL

Chop all the fruit except grapes into 1-inch (2.5-cm) pieces. Cut the grapes in half. Toss immediately in a large bowl with lemon or lime juice to prevent the fruit from browning.

Add the Grand Marnier and cinnamon and combine well. Serve with sweetened whipped cream or Vanilla Cream Topping (p. 162).

Grasshopper Sandwiches

The idea for this easy, stylish dessert came from two places. The first was my collection of cookbooks from the '50s and '60s in which ice cream drizzled with crème de menthe was often suggested for a quick dessert. Then, my partner in crime, Ilana, remembered a Grasshopper Pie that her mom used to make, consisting of a crushed chocolate wafer crust filled with minty marshmallow filling.

Makes 15-20 sandwiches

2^1/$_2$ cups	vanilla ice cream	625 mL
2^1/$_2$ tsp.	green crème de menthe	12.5 mL
1	7-oz. (200-g) package chocolate wafers	1

In a medium bowl, mix together the ice cream and crème de menthe. Transfer to a container with a tight-fitting lid and freeze for at least 2 hours.

To put together the sandwiches, you need to work quickly. Start by putting a large dish in the freezer. Remove the ice cream from the freezer and put about a tablespoon of ice cream on the rough side of a wafer; you want the smooth sides out. Press a second wafer on top of this, using a knife to smooth around the edges. Continue until all of your ice cream is used up, putting each sandwich in the freezer as you make it.

Cover the sandwiches and freeze for at least 4 hours. They are best if they're frozen overnight.

Custard Sauce (Crème Anglaise)

A homemade custard sauce is a wonderful addition to many of the desserts in this book. Like Custard Pudding (p. 190), this does take time and some patience, but it's not difficult to make. Drizzle over hot puddings and crumbles, and on the plate beside pies and cakes.

Makes about 3 cups (750 mL)

2^1/$_2$ cups	milk	625 mL
4	egg yolks	4
^{1}/$_3$ cup	sugar	80 mL
pinch	salt	pinch
^{1}/$_2$ tsp.	vanilla	2.5 mL

Heat the milk until hot, but don't let it boil. While the milk heats, beat the egg yolks lightly in a large glass or metal bowl—you will be setting it over a pan of simmering water, so it must be heatproof (not plastic). Beat in the sugar, then the salt.

Slowly add the hot milk to the egg mixture in a steady stream, whisking constantly. Set the bowl over a saucepan of simmering, *not* rapidly boiling, water. Make sure that the bottom of the bowl is not touching the water; otherwise the custard will overcook and separate.

Heat the custard, stirring occasionally for the first 10 minutes, then with increasing frequency as it starts to thicken during the next 7–10 minutes, and then constantly for the last 5–10 minutes. Continue to heat the custard until it has thickened to the point where it coats your spoon. Once it does this, remove it from the heat *immediately*.

Stir in the vanilla and chill thoroughly.

All-Purpose Frosting

This versatile buttercream frosting is great for birthdays and special occasions such as Valentine's Day, as it can be tinted very easily with a few drops of food coloring. If you are talented and patient, it also pipes well—you might want to add about $^1/_2$ cup (125 mL) extra icing sugar to get a stiffer consistency. This frosting is rich, buttery, and it also works very well with a good vegan margarine and soymilk.

Makes about 2 cups (500 mL) icing, enough for 2 cake layers or 24 cupcakes

$^1/_4$ cup	butter, softened	60 mL
1 tsp.	vanilla	5 mL
5 Tbsp.	milk	75 mL
5–5$^1/_2$ cups	icing sugar	1.25–1.4 L

With an electric mixer or a strong arm, beat the butter and vanilla together in a large bowl. Add the milk and icing sugar alternately—the milk in tablespoon (15-mL) increments, and the icing sugar in $^1/_2$-cup (125-mL) increments—blending thoroughly after each addition.

When you reach 5 cups (1.25 L) of icing sugar, add more icing sugar slowly until you reach a spreadable consistency that forms a soft peak when you pull a spoon upward through it.

Spread on cooled cakes or cupcakes as is, or tint with 2–3 drops of food coloring. For cupcakes, you can divide the icing into 3 or 4 bowls and tint each a different color for variety.

Orange or Lemon Frosting:

Omit the vanilla and milk. Instead of milk, use 5 Tbsp. (75 mL) orange or lemon juice, and, if desired, replace the vanilla with $1/2$ tsp. (2.5 mL) orange or lemon extract. You can tint the icing with food coloring— 2 drops each of red and yellow for orange, and 2–3 drops of yellow for lemon.

Cherry Frosting:

Perfect for the one you love. Add $1/4$ cup (60 mL) finely chopped red maraschino cherries to the icing, as well as 2–3 drops of red food coloring for a pink color.

Chocolate or Mocha Frosting:

Increase the butter by 1 Tbsp. (15 mL). Add $1/4$–$1/3$ cup (60–80 mL) cocoa with the icing sugar—use the quantity you need to reach the chocolate taste you like. You may need to decrease the amount of icing sugar slightly. For mocha, substitute 3 Tbsp. (45 mL) of the milk with strong, black, cold coffee or espresso.

Peppermint Frosting:

Omit the vanilla and use 1 tsp. (5 mL) peppermint extract instead. Use 2–3 drops of green food coloring to make a light green color. Add $1/4$ cup (60 mL) crushed peppermint candies or candy canes, if desired.

Key Lime Cheesecake

I created this dessert to pair my love for Key Lime Pie with my desire to lighten up the taste of the conventional cheesecake. With its chocolate crust, tart filling, and creamy topping, I think you'll find it's a success on both fronts. The end result is absolutely mouthwatering. Make this a day ahead, because it does need to chill overnight.

Makes one 10-inch (25-cm) cheesecake

1^1/3 cups	chocolate wafer crumbs	330 mL
^{1}/3 cup	butter, melted	80 mL
3	8.8-oz. (250-g) packages cream cheese, softened	3
1^1/2 cups	ricotta	375 mL
1^1/4 cups	granulated sugar	300 mL
1 tsp.	vanilla extract	5 mL
3	eggs	3
^{1}/4 cup + 3 Tbsp.	lime juice, strained	105 mL
1 Tbsp.	finely grated lime rind (5–6 limes, including 1 lime for garnish)	15 mL
2 cups	sour cream	500 mL
	extra sugar and lime for garnish	

Preheat to oven to 350°F (175°C). In a medium bowl, mix together the chocolate wafer crumbs and melted butter until thoroughly combined.

Butter the bottom and sides of a 10-inch (25-cm) springform pan. Press the crumb mixture evenly into the pan, covering the bottom and ^{1}/2 inch (1 cm) up the sides. Bake for 6 minutes just to set the crust. Remove the crust from the oven and let cool. Keep the oven temperature at 350°F (175°C).

In a large bowl, beat the cream cheese with an electric mixer until smooth. In a blender or food processor, purée the ricotta on high speed until it's completely smooth, 1–2 minutes, scraping down the sides with a rubber scraper at least once. Add the creamed ricotta to the cream cheese and mix until thoroughly combined.

As you add ingredients to the cream cheese, scrape down the sides of your bowl frequently.

Beat in 1 cup (250 mL) of the sugar, then add the vanilla. Beat in the eggs 1 at a time until completely smooth and uniform. Beat in all but 1 Tbsp. (15 mL) of the lime juice, and all of the lime rind.

Pour the mixture into the springform pan and spread evenly. Bake at the center of your oven for 1 hour, and don't open the oven door during this time. Mix up the sour cream topping before the hour is up.

For the topping, beat together the sour cream with the remaining ¼ cup (60 mL) sugar and 1 Tbsp. (15 mL) lime juice.

When the cheesecake has baked for 1 hour, remove it and immediately increase the oven temperature to 450°F (230°C). Run a knife around the sides of the cheesecake, cleaning the knife off partway through if necessary, then pour the sour cream topping over top. As soon as the oven reaches 450°F (230°C), return the cheesecake to the oven and bake for 5 minutes. Turn the heat off and let the cheesecake cool in the oven with the door slightly open for 1½ hours. This discourages the surface of the cheesecake from cracking.

Remove the cheesecake from the oven and let it reach room temperature if it hasn't already. Chill in the refrigerator for at least 8 hours—it's best to leave it overnight.

Before serving, garnish the cheesecake with thin lime slices that you've coated with sugar—I like to do a ring of slices around the outside. If you have any cracks in the surface, use the lime slices to cover them up. Run a knife around the sides of the cheesecake once more, stopping to clean the knife off if necessary. Carefully unhinge and remove the sides of the pan. Serve.

Cheesecake, as a rule, is not for dieters, but if you want a little less guilt, you can use low-fat ricotta and 1 package of light cream cheese with 2 packages of regular. You can also use low-fat sour cream for the topping.

Vegan Chocolate-Rum Cheesecake

This is a stupendous dessert whether you're vegan or not. I'm definitely an advocate of silken tofu in desserts—it has a lovely texture for puddings and fillings—but I do believe it has to be tarted up and flavored. This dish is best made one day in advance, as it should chill thoroughly.

Makes one 10-inch (25-cm) cheesecake

1^1/$_2$ cups	vegan graham cracker crumbs	375 mL
1^1/$_2$ cups	packed brown sugar	375 mL
pinch	salt	pinch
^{1}/$_3$ cup	butter or vegan margarine, melted	80 mL
2	12-oz. (340-mL) boxes soft silken tofu, drained	2
1	12-oz. (340-mL) box firm silken tofu, drained	1
^{1}/$_2$ cup + 3 Tbsp.	cocoa powder	170 mL
1 Tbsp.	vanilla extract	15 mL
^{1}/$_4$ cup + 1 Tbsp.	dark rum	75 mL
^{1}/$_4$ cup + 2 Tbsp.	peanut oil	90 mL
	fresh raspberries for garnish (optional)	
1 batch	Raspberry Sauce (p. 162)	1 batch

Preheat the oven to 350˚F (175˚C). In a medium bowl, mix together the graham crumbs, ^{1}/$_4$ cup (60 mL) brown sugar, and salt. Add the melted butter or margarine and use your fingers to work it into the crumbs.

Grease the bottom and sides of a 10-inch (25-cm) springform pan with butter or margarine. Press the crumb mixture evenly into the pan, covering the bottom and going ^{1}/$_2$–1 inch (1–2.5 cm) up the sides. Bake for 6 minutes just to set the crust. Remove the crust from the oven and reduce the heat to 325˚F (165˚C).

Put the tofu, cocoa, vanilla, rum, peanut oil, and remaining 1^1/$_4$ cups (300 mL) brown sugar into a food processor or blender. Purée until it is completely smooth and you can't see any little white bits of tofu—stop and scrape down the sides of the container at least once as you purée.

Pour the filling into the graham crust, using a rubber scraper or spatula to spread the mixture evenly, making sure the sides of the graham crust are covered. Bake, uncovered, for 1 hour and 15 minutes. Turn the heat off and let the cheesecake cool in the oven with the door slightly open for 1^1/$_2$ hours. This discourages the surface of the cheesecake from cracking.

Remove the cheesecake from the oven and let it reach room temperature if it hasn't already.

Refrigerate the cheesecake for at least 6 hours, but preferably overnight. Run a clean butter knife around the cake to loosen it from the pan, removing the knife a few times and cleaning it as you go. Unhinge the sides and carefully remove from the cheesecake.

Place the cheesecake on a platter and garnish with fresh raspberries, if you like. As you serve, drizzle each person's plate liberally with Raspberry Sauce (p. 162).

Your grocery or health food store should carry Mori-Nu tofu, which has patented the boxes mentioned in the ingredients for this recipe and is one of the most widely available brands of tofu. These boxes, which look similar to drinking boxes, are extremely convenient because they're vacuum-packed and have a shelf life of months and months. Mori-Nu also makes a distinction between different categories of silken tofu, from firm to extra-soft, whereas most other companies use the moniker "silken" only for soft tofu. It may also be available in low-fat, but buy the regular kind for cheesecake.

If you can't find silken tofu, do this: buy enough soft tofu to fit the bill for the "soft silken tofu" requirement, then buy enough firm tofu for the "firm silken tofu" requirement. It should work just the same.

One-Pan Wonder Cake

My friend Margaret and I used to make this cake when we were kids, staying over at each other's houses on Friday nights. We called it "Wacky Cake." A few years ago, I talked to someone else who knew it as "Crazy Cake." And, in *The I Hate to Cook Book* Peg Bracken makes a variation of this that she calls "Cockeyed Cake." Whatever you call it, it's a bit of a legend—and it's vegan.

Makes one 9-inch (23-cm) square cake

1 1/2 cups	all-purpose flour	375 mL
1/4 cup	cocoa	60 mL
1 tsp.	baking soda	5 mL
1 cup	white sugar	250 mL
1/2 tsp.	salt	2.5 mL
1/4 cup	vegetable oil	60 mL
1 Tbsp.	vinegar	15 mL
1 tsp.	vanilla	5 mL
1 cup	cold water	250 mL

Preheat the oven to 350°F (175°C). Grease a 9-inch (23-cm) square baking pan, and sift the flour, cocoa, baking soda, sugar, and salt right into the pan. Spread the mixture out evenly.

With a fork, make 3 holes in the flour mixture. Pour the oil in the first, the vinegar in the second, and the vanilla in the third. Pour the water over the whole mess and mix together with a fork or spoon, making sure that you get the stuff in the corners of the pan. Mix until combined, but a few small lumps are all right. Don't overmix.

Bake for about 30 minutes, or until a knife inserted in the center comes out clean. Cool and frost with All-Purpose Frosting (p. 178).

Cherries Jubilee

I had always heard of Cherries Jubilee from people of my parents' generation who seldom made it themselves, but often ordered it or saw it being served at restaurants in the '60s. It's a real showcase dessert, extremely flashy and impressive. It's also delicious and very easy. Safety note: don't drink too much of the kirsch before setting it on fire.

Serves 4

1	14-oz. (398-mL) can Bing cherries	1
1 tsp.	cornstarch	5 mL
1/2 tsp.	grated lemon rind	2.5 mL
2 Tbsp.	sugar	30 mL
2 Tbsp.	orange juice	30 mL
2 Tbsp. + 2 tsp.	kirsch	40 mL
8 scoops	vanilla ice cream or frozen yogurt	8 scoops

Drain the cherries over your blender or food processor. Transfer the drained cherries to a medium saucepan. Add the cornstarch, lemon rind, sugar, and orange juice to the cherry liquid, and blend until smooth, 20–30 seconds.

Add the blended liquid to the cherries, and bring to a boil over medium-high heat. Simmer for about 5 minutes, or until the sauce has thickened. At this point, make sure that your ice cream is ready to serve and have all the bowls and spoons ready for your guests.

Heat the kirsch in a small pan over low heat—you can tell it's hot when you start to see ribbons of steam rising from it. While the kirsch is heating, put 2 scoops of ice cream in each bowl.

When the kirsch is hot, turn off the heat under the kirsch and cherries, and quickly transfer the cherries to a shallow, heatproof serving dish. Light a match and barely touch it to the side of the kirsch—this will create a blue flame. Immediately pour the kirsch over the cherries and serve—the flame will go out within a minute.

When the flame goes out, spoon cherries and sauce over each person's bowl of ice cream.

Sherry Trifle #1

Fruity, delectable cake, rich custard, smooth cream, and tart raspberries. This dessert does take some time and effort, but I can tell you
that it's probably my very favorite—and it's very beautiful as well. In
fact, I think trifle is so important that I've included two versions of it:
my dad's and my mom's. This one is my dad's.

Serves 6–8

1	3-oz. (85-g) box raspberry-flavored kosher gel dessert	1
2 cups	white cake of any kind, cut into 2-inch (5-cm) strips, packed	500 mL
2 tsp.	sherry	10 mL
1 batch	Custard Pudding (p. 190), not chilled	1 batch
1 1/2 cups	whipping cream	375 mL
3–4 Tbsp.	sugar	45–60 mL
1 1/2 cups	raspberries	375 mL

Layer 1: empty the gel powder into a large, heatproof, transparent
glass bowl (this is a dessert that contains beautiful layers, so it looks
best in a bowl you can see through). Add the amount of boiling water
specified on the box. Add cake strips and use a spoon to press them
down into the gel so they're saturated. Chill to set, but when the gel
is about half set, drizzle 1 tsp. (5 mL) of the sherry on top.

Layer 2: prepare the custard pudding according to the directions, but
pour it on top of the cake layer when the custard is lukewarm—this
way, it will set as a layer on top of the cake. Spread evenly over top.
Chill to set.

Layer 3: put a large bowl and the beaters from your electric mixer into the freezer to chill. When chilled, remove from the freezer and pour in the whipping cream. Beat on high speed until soft peaks form, 4–5 minutes. Add 3 Tbsp. (45 mL) sugar and beat for 1–2 minutes more, scraping down the sides of the bowl halfway through.

In a small bowl, stir together the raspberries and 1 tsp.–1 Tbsp. (5–15 mL) sugar—you want the raspberries to be a bit tart, and the amount of sugar you need depends upon the sweetness of your raspberries. Toss in the remaining 1 tsp. (5 mL) sherry. Set aside.

Mound the whipped cream in a ring on top of the custard, so there is a hole in the center. Spoon the raspberries into the center, drizzling any sherry syrup from the raspberries over top.

To serve, use a large spoon to dig into the trifle, so that each person gets to taste all of the layers.

Why kosher gel? Unfortunately, the gelatin dessert we all grew up with is made with just that—gelatin, a gelling agent made from animal by-products. Happily, I've found a vegetarian alternative in the Jewish food aisle at my local supermarket, called "kosher gel dessert." It's just as easy to make, and has the same retro taste as the original. Kosher gel that is marked "pareve" contains no meat or milk, so it is permissible for Jewish people—and vegetarians—to eat with any meal.

Sherry Trifle #2

This is the trifle to make if you can't find kosher gel dessert, or if you just don't feel like using it. Be aware that this is also the more uppercrust version of trifle, so dust off your Ascots and fine china before eating.

Serves 6–8

1 batch	Custard Pudding (p. 190), made with 1 extra egg yolk, and 1 extra 1/2 cup (125 mL) milk	1 batch
3 cups	raspberries, sliced strawberries, or a combination of the two	750 mL
6 Tbsp.	sugar (approx.)	90 mL
3 Tbsp.	sherry	45 mL
4 cups	white cake of any kind, cut into 2-inch (5-cm) strips, packed	1 L
1 1/2 cups	whipping cream	375 mL

Prepare the custard according to the directions, adding the extra egg yolk and milk. Set aside to cool to lukewarm or room temperature— but don't let it cool completely, as it will set.

In a medium bowl, mix the berries with about 3 Tbsp. (45 mL) sugar— a little more or less to taste. You want the berries to be a bit tart. Add 1 Tbsp. (15 mL) sherry, and let sit for at least 10 minutes, stirring occasionally. This will help form a syrup.

In a large bowl, drizzle 1 Tbsp. (15 mL) sherry over the cake strips. Put half of the cake into the bottom of a large, transparent glass bowl (this is a dessert that contains beautiful layers, so it looks best in a bowl you can see through).

Spread about ³/₄ cup (185 mL) berries over the cake, drizzling some syrup over as well. Then spread half of the custard over the berries, using a spoon or spatula to spread it evenly.

Repeat the cake/berries/custard layers once more. You should have a custard layer on top and some berries left over. Chill the trifle to set.

As the trifle is chilling, whip the cream. Put a large bowl and the beaters from your electric mixer into the freezer to chill. When chilled, remove from the freezer and pour in the whipping cream. Beat on high speed until soft peaks form, 4–5 minutes. Add 3 Tbsp. (45 mL) sugar and beat for 1–2 minutes more, scraping down the sides of the bowl halfway through.

Once the trifle has set slightly (about 30 minutes), mound the whipped cream in a ring on top of the custard, so there is a hole in the center. Spoon the remaining berries into the center, drizzling any sherry syrup from the berries over top. Chill for at least 30 minutes more.

To serve, use a large spoon to dig into the trifle, so that each person gets to taste all of the layers.

Custard Pudding

Custard is so unbelievably good when it's made from scratch. The trick to making a good custard is to heat it very slowly—once you've mastered this, the rest isn't difficult. Enjoy it on its own, with a little whipped cream, or as a topping for fresh or stewed fruit.

Makes about 3 cups (750 mL)

2 cups	milk	500 mL
3	eggs	3
1/3 cup	sugar	125 mL
pinch	salt	pinch
1/2 tsp.	vanilla	2.5 mL

Heat the milk until hot, but don't let it boil. While the milk heats, beat the eggs lightly in a large glass or metal bowl—you will be setting it over a pan of simmering water, so it must be heatproof (not plastic). Beat in the sugar, then the salt.

Slowly add the hot milk to the egg mixture in a steady stream, whisking constantly. Set the bowl over a saucepan of simmering, *not* rapidly boiling, water. Make sure that the bottom of the bowl is not touching the water; otherwise the custard will overcook and separate.

Heat the custard, stirring occasionally for the first 10 minutes, then with increasing frequency as it starts to thicken during the next 7–10 minutes, and then constantly for the last 5–10 minutes. Continue to heat the custard until it has thickened to the point where it thickly coats your spoon. Once it does this, remove it from the heat *immediately*.

Stir in the vanilla and pour into individual serving dishes, if desired. Chill to set.

Rice Pudding

This pudding, the real thing, is a great dessert for a cold winter night, and it's very nutritious. My favorite way to eat it is hot out of the oven with jam on top—or try whipping up Raspberry Sauce (p. 162) to drizzle over.

Makes one 8- x 11-inch (20- x 28-cm) pan

³/₄ cup	short-grain Italian rice (Arborio)	185 mL
¹/₂ cup	white sugar	125 mL
³/₄ tsp.	freshly grated nutmeg, or 1 tsp. (5 mL) ground nutmeg	4 mL
5 cups	milk	1.25 L
1 Tbsp.	butter	15 mL

Preheat the oven to 325°F (165°C). Put the rice into a colander and rinse under cold water for about 30 seconds; you don't want the water to run clear. Drain and empty into an 8- x 11-inch (20- x 28-cm) dish, spreading it out evenly. Sprinkle the sugar and nutmeg evenly over top. Pour the milk over, and drop the butter in small bits all over the surface.

Bake for about an hour, or until the milk has been absorbed and the pudding has started to brown on top. Serve warm.

You should be able to find whole nutmeg at a bulk spice store or a gourmet cooking shop. Do try to find it; grating it yourself is extremely easy and it perfumes your kitchen. Grate it using the finest setting of your grater.

Bananas Jennifer

. . . So named because they're my version of "Bananas Patricia," a dessert that my dad created for my mom and kept on the restaurant menu for a long time. This is a quick and easy dessert that tastes classy and absolutely fantastic. Don't skip the rum.

Serves 4-6

2	eggs	2
$1/2$ tsp.	vanilla extract	2.5 mL
$1/2$ cup	milk	125 mL
1 cup	graham cracker crumbs	250 mL
$1/2$ cup	all-purpose flour	125 mL
$1/4$ tsp.	cinnamon	1.2 mL
4	large ripe bananas	4
$1/3$–$1/2$ cup	butter	80–125 mL
4–6 scoops	vanilla ice cream	4–6 scoops
2–3 Tbsp.	dark rum	30–45 mL

Beat the eggs lightly in a small bowl. Beat in the vanilla and milk. Set aside.

In a large, shallow bowl, combine the graham crumbs, $1/4$ cup (60 mL) flour, and cinnamon. Set aside.

Put the remaining flour into a small bowl. Set aside.

Peel the bananas and slice each banana into 8 pieces like this: cut the banana in half lengthwise, then crosswise. This will give you 4 quarters. Then, cut each quarter in half lengthwise so that you create 8 "spears."

Dip 2 or 3 spears first in the flour bowl, coating lightly with flour. Shake excess flour off gently and then dip into the egg wash, coating thoroughly. Transfer to the graham cracker bowl and toss the spears until thoroughly coated. Repeat with all the banana spears.

Melt about $1/4$ cup (60 mL) butter over medium-high heat in a large skillet—you will be shallow-frying the banana and may need slightly more butter if your skillet is not non-stick. Don't scrimp on the butter, as you need enough fat to crisp up the coating.

When the butter is melted and the skillet is hot, add about half the banana spears. Fry, turning or tossing bananas in the skillet, until all sides are browned, about 5 minutes total. Transfer to paper towels to drain excess fat. Put the first batch of cooked spears on a baking sheet in a 200°F (95°C) oven to keep warm. Repeat until all the bananas are done.

To serve, put 1 scoop of ice cream onto the middle of each person's dish or shallow bowl. Stack 6–8 banana spears vertically all around the ice cream, as if you were building a teepee. Drizzle each serving with about $1/2$ Tbsp. (7.5 mL) rum. Serve immediately.

Here's a lesson I was taught over a flaming Christmas pudding: whenever you're heating alcohol or adding it to any pot on the stove, never add it from the bottle. Pour it into a thick shot glass or something similar first. This is to prevent the bottle of alcohol from exploding due to the heat. Your safest bet, in fact, is to add alcohol to a pan well away from the stove and then move the pan onto the stove, rather than ever pouring alcohol near the stove.

glossary of ingredients & cooking terms

Bulgur:

Also spelled "bulghur" and "bulgar," bulgur is made from wheat kernels that are steamed, then dried and crushed. It is used widely in Middle Eastern dishes. Bulgur needs to be hydrated before it is eaten. It comes in fine, medium, or coarse consistencies—for pilafs and most other savory dishes, medium or coarse is best.

Chili paste:

Widely used in Asian dishes, chili paste can be found in most supermarkets. Sambal Oelek is a popular Indonesian version. It always contains chili peppers, and may also contain vinegar, garlic, and various spices, depending on the brand.

Coulis:

This term comes from the French verb *couler*, meaning "to flow." As such, a coulis refers to a puréed sauce that is thin enough to pour.

Crimini mushrooms:

The same shape and size as regular white button mushrooms, these have a darker-colored cap and a deeper, earthier flavor. They can be substituted for white mushrooms, but expect a more "mushroomy" taste.

Crostini:

An Italian term for "little toasts," it is just that: small slices of bread that are usually brushed with olive oil and then grilled or toasted. Crostini are an excellent carrier for all kinds of dips and side dishes, such as Bruschetta (p. 146) and Faux Gras (p. 141).

Gluten flour:

This is made from whole wheat flour that is treated to remove most of the carbohydrate, leaving the gluten behind. Gluten is a mixture of proteins that makes dough stick together and become elastic. As such, gluten flour aids the cohesion of ingredients.

Hoisin sauce:

Used as a condiment with a lot of Asian dishes, hoisin sauce is very thick and has a sweet, salty taste. Hoisin is available in most supermarkets, but try to find one that doesn't contain MSG, to save yourself a headache.

Kirsch:

Also called "kirschwasser," this is a clear brandy made from cherries. The name is German: *kirsch* (cherry) and *wasser* (water). A spoonful makes a wonderful addition to many cocktails. In the food world, kirsch is most commonly used for Cherries Jubilee (p. 185).

Kosher:

This term refers to food that is prepared according to Jewish laws.
See also *Pareve*.

Marmite:

This yeast concentrate paste is spread very thinly on toast and used in stocks and gravies. Once known only to Brits, this great vegetarian product, which is rich in B vitamins, has found its way onto supermarket shelves everywhere. If Marmite cannot be found, its Australian rival, Vegemite, can also be used.

MSG:

Monosodium glutamate is a flavor enhancer that is added to many soups and soup stock powders, sauces, and other foods. MSG is the sodium salt of glutamate, and glutamate is an amino acid that occurs naturally in protein-rich foods. MSG enhances the taste of foods by mimicking the natural reaction you would have if you were eating a glutamate-rich food. Some people have no adverse reactions whatsoever to MSG, but others can suffer headaches, flushing, nausea, and dizzy spells. I always get a headache and so avoid it whenever I can.

Natural peanut butter:

This is peanut butter made just from peanuts. It can be found at any health food store—some stores have a fun machine that lets you grind your own peanut butter right then and there. Natural peanut butter is increasingly available at the supermarket as well. People are always going on about how high in fat peanut butter is, and if you look at conventional brands, you can see why—they're loaded with shortening, sugar, and other unnecessary things. Because natural peanut butter has no preservatives, you should keep it refrigerated once it's opened.

Nutritional yeast flakes:

Nutritional yeast flakes, also called "good-tasting yeast flakes," are an inactive yeast food supplement. They have two distinct benefits in vegetarian cooking. First, they are an excellent source of B vitamins. Second, they add a wonderful, rich, cheese-like flavor to foods. If you're vegetarian, and especially if you're vegan, nutritional yeast flakes should be a staple in your pantry. As well as using them in many recipes in this book, try sprinkling these flakes over pizza or pasta as a cheese substitute.

Oyster mushrooms:

These don't look like traditional mushrooms; they look more like tan-colored elephant ears. These mushrooms have a lovely, delicate flavor, and are best sautéed in butter with a little onion.

Pareve or parve:

Vegan alert! This term refers to a food that contains neither meat nor milk—it's a designation that tells Jewish people that they can eat the food with meat or milk (so as to comply with Jewish law, which states that meat and milk can't be eaten together). The only thing you have to look for on the label is eggs—pareve foods can have eggs in them.

Pith:

This is the spongy, white tissue between the peel of a citrus fruit and the fruit itself. When using peeled citrus fruit in recipes, it's important to remove as much pith as possible, as it has a very bitter taste.

Portobello mushrooms:

These mushrooms are much larger than regular white button mushrooms, and have a much heftier price tag. But they're worth it—sliced thinly and grilled, they become a hearty cutlet or burger in and of themselves, with a wonderfully dark, meaty taste.

Roux:

This is a mixture of flour and fat (usually butter) that is used to thicken sauces.

Silken tofu:

See *Tofu*.

Swede:

Called "rutabagas" in North America and "neeps" in Scotland, swedes are like large turnips. In fact, they are called "swede" because the word "rutabaga" has a Swedish derivation. These large, round root vegetables usually have a yellowish skin on top and a purple skin on the bottom. Part of the cruciferous family of vegetables, they are a source of vitamins A and C. They have a slightly sweet, peppery taste and are delicious boiled and mashed. Store swedes in a cool, dry place.

Tahini:

A very rich paste made from sesame seeds, tahini is used in Middle Eastern foods, and a little goes a long way.

Tofu:

A protein-rich vegetarian food made from soybean curd, tofu has been much-maligned in North America in the past. However, it is starting to gain wide acceptance due to its strong nutritional attributes and its versatility. Tofu is available in a range of textures.

Extra-firm tofu is hard and crumbly, almost like feta cheese. It is an excellent substitute for eggs in scrambles and egg salads, and it's great in stir-fries and marinades if you don't like your tofu soft and "mushy."

Firm tofu generally has a smoother, silkier feel in the mouth than extra-firm, but still holds its shape in dishes.

Soft tofu does not hold its shape when cut into pieces, but its soft creamy texture makes it perfect for desserts such as mousses and puddings.

Silken tofu generally refers to soft tofu, but some companies, such as Mori-Nu, use the term for a whole range of tofu, from firm to extra-soft.

TVP:

Short for "Texturized Vegetable Protein" and made from soy flour, TVP is an excellent vegetarian food. It's high in protein and fiber, and has almost no fat. It is now found in health food stores, bulk stores, and most supermarkets. However, buy in bulk if you can. I've noticed the packaged stuff is often triple the price! Hot water or cooking liquids must be added, as it is a dehydrated product. TVP comes in several different forms, and they're not always labelled consistently. Use your good judgment and the following guidelines to determine which kind you need to take home with you.

TVP chunks look just like they sound—chunks about 3/4 inch (2 cm) around. They rehydrate into bite-sized pieces for stir-fries and stews.

TVP flakes are generally about 1 inch (2.5 cm) long and 1/2 inch (1 cm) thick. They rehydrate into pieces that can be marinated and thrown into stir-fries, or made into kebabs with vegetables. They are a good substitute for TVP chunks.

TVP granules look like dehydrated ground meat, and they rehydrate to the uncanny texture and appearance of cooked ground meat. TVP granules are the most creatively labelled of the three types; sometimes they're just called "TVP," and sometimes they're confusingly called "flakes." But no matter what your store calls the stuff, what you're looking for is this ground-meat-like texture. TVP granules are extremely versatile. They can be added to chilis or pasta sauces, or rehydrated and mixed with a binder for burgers.

Vegetarian oyster sauce:

This salty, thick sauce is made with mushrooms rather than oysters and is used in stir-fries and other Asian dishes. It's widely available in Asian markets, and quite a few regular grocery stores now carry it, too.

Vidalia onion:

This onion is the Official State Vegetable of Georgia, and is named after the town where it was first sold at a farmer's market in the 1940s. When you see Vidalias in your farmer's market or grocery store in the summertime, buy them up and take advantage. They're beautifully sweet, mild onions that can be eaten raw with no trepidation. They're also fantastic for French Onion Soup (p. 62)—just omit the sugar.

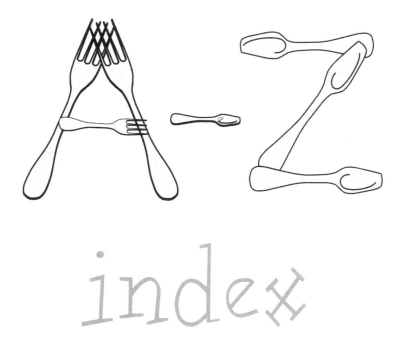

index

Born in Ottawa, Ontario, Jennifer Warren grew up in Port Sydney where her parents owned a restaurant. She spent her childhood in the kitchen watching her mom and dad cook for their customers. She developed a love of comfort food that was drastically curtailed when she became vegetarian as a teenager. Since then, she has experimented with a wide range of recipes—and the help of family, friends and her cats as taste-testers—to re-create the dishes of her youth without the meat.

Jennifer attended Trent University where she studied philosophy and English literature. She also studied creative writing with Orm Mitchell, son of W.O. Mitchell, and continues to write short stories. She now works as a writer and editor, and is currently creating recipes for a series of dinner-themed CDs.

Jennifer collects vintage cookbooks and cocktail books. She is guiltily addicted to pop culture and can hum almost any song—no matter how obscure or cheesy. She lives with her partner and her two cats in Montreal, Quebec.